The unmailed letter to Justice Douglas

THE WHITE HOUSE
WASHINGTON

July 9, 1952

Dear Bill:

I appreciated very much your letter of July third and
I am sorry that I didn't have a chance to talk with you
before you left. In fact, I am sorry that I didn't have
an opportunity to discuss precedents with you before
you came to the conclusion you did on that crazy decision that has tied up the country.

I am writing a monograph on just what makes Justices
of the Supreme Court tick. There was no decision by
the majority although there were seven opinions against
what was best for the country.

I don't see how a Court made up of so-called "Liberals"
could do what that Court did to me. I am going to find
out just why before I quit this office.

Sincerely yours,

Harry S. Truman

Honorable William O. Douglas
Justice of the Supreme Court
Washington 13, D. C.

STRICTLY PERSONAL AND CONFIDENTIAL

The Letters Harry Truman Never Mailed

STRICTLY PERSONAL AND CONFIDENTIAL

The Letters Harry Truman Never Mailed

EDITED BY
Monte M. Poen

Little, Brown and Company Boston / Toronto

FIRST EDITION

Library of Congress Cataloging in Publication Data

Truman, Harry S., 1884–1972.
    Strictly personal and confidential.

    Includes bibliographical references and index.
    1. Truman, Harry S., 1884–1972. 2. Presidents—United States—Corre-
spondence. I. Poen, Monte M., 1930– . II. Title.
E814.A4 1982b 973.918′092′4 81–20879
ISBN 0–316–71221–3   AACR2

MV

Designed by Janis Capone

Published simultaneously in Canada
by Little, Brown & Company (Canada) Limited

PRINTED IN THE UNITED STATES OF AMERICA

CONTENTS

		About the Editing	ix
		Acknowledgments	xi
I		Harry Truman, Letter Writer	3
	II	The Press	9
III		The War, the A-Bomb, & After	31
	IV	Stopping Reds in Asia	49
	V	Running the Government	61
VI		Human Greed and Human Need	85
	VII	Democrats or High Hats?	107
	VIII	Harry Truman, Historian	138
IX		Kinfolk, Neighbors, and Others	170
		Source Notes	187
		Index	199

ABOUT THE EDITING

Harry Truman was a literate man. He liked to write and he knew how to communicate his thoughts with an economy of words. So, other than introductory comments, my compilation of the letters he never mailed needed little editorial clarification. To avoid confusion or distraction, I did correct occasional misspelling; while Mr. Truman was not a poor speller, he understandably ignored grammatical precision when penning a fiery letter.

Some of the letters lacked dates or had a first-name-only salutation, and this required more than usual background research. For example, a missing date made it difficult to pin down the story that triggered the President's angry memo to the publisher of *American Aviation* magazine (page 26). To do so, I had to travel to the University of Iowa to search through its collection of scarce thirty-year-old copies of that magazine. Also, the omitted surname from a letter addressed "Dear Bill" (page 151) remains a mystery; Harry Truman, it turned out, corresponded with dozens of people named Bill. Most of the time, however, this missing information could be surmised from related letters, memos, or news clippings I found in Truman's private papers at the Harry S. Truman Library in Independence, Missouri.

As for how I determined that a Truman letter was not sent, the evidence was usually explicit. Either an attached notation revealed that the President had decided to withhold it, or a copy of a substitute letter was in the files. Only Truman's handwritten letters posed a problem. I finally concluded that a number of them were messy duplicates of letters the President later cleaned up for mailing. These, of course, I dropped from my original list of "unmailed" letters, and they do not appear in the book.

ACKNOWLEDGMENTS

My previous trips to the Harry S. Truman Library in Independence, Missouri, were pleasant and productive, but the eleven months I lived in Independence researching and editing this book were something special. The excitement over discovering new Truman materials, the uninterrupted time for working with them, the getting back in touch with my Midwestern beginnings, the pleasure of becoming acquainted with President Truman's kinfolk and with his hometown neighbors, the making of new friends — all of these experiences helped me overcome a severe case of "what else is new?" middle-age blahs.

I am most indebted to the Truman Library's competent staff. From Library director Benedict K. Zobrist on down, they could not have been more hospitable or helpful. I worked most closely with research archivist Erwin Mueller and with librarian Elizabeth Safly, and to them I owe a special thanks. Erwin, with his phenomenal ability to recall in what file, in what box, in what folder I might find missing information, helped immeasurably. Elizabeth, if she couldn't answer one of my all-too-frequent questions by consulting her research room references, cheerfully picked up the phone and got the answer from someone she knew in the Kansas City area. Niel

Johnson provided willing assistance in photocopying documents. Vicky Alexander, Dennis Bilger, Patty Bressman, Robin Burgess, Mildred Carol, Donna Clark, Harry Clark, John Curry, James Fuchs, Philip Lagerquist, Warren Ohrvall, Doris Pesek, and Pauline Testerman contributed in various ways.

Don Drummond, owner of the Beauty Rest Motel, where I normally stay during my shorter visits to Independence, unselfishly helped me locate more permanent lodging. Likewise, R. Gordon Tompkins, from whom I ultimately rented an apartment, treated me more like a friend than as a tenant. Midwesterners are warmhearted and generous people.

Fellow historians also helped. Robert H. Ferrell of Indiana University, who recently edited a highly significant volume of Mr. Truman's handwritten private papers, shared his recollections on the ins and outs of publishing this type of book. Franklin D. Mitchell of the University of Southern California, and Dwight E. Mayo, a colleague at Northern Arizona University, read an early draft and rendered valuable critiques. Moreover, Dwight handled important on-campus matters for me during my absence from NAU.

My son Gregory and another friend, Clinton Reynolds, pointed out some pedagogical distractions, including some overly detailed editorial explanations, thereby helping me overcome ingrained professorial habits. Peggy Freudenthal, alert and skillful copyeditor at Little, Brown, identified other places where confusion lurked.

Of course, this whole enterprise owes a great deal to the sabbatical leave and to the other forms of research assistance I received from Northern Arizona University. A grant-in-aid from the Harry S. Truman Library Institute also helped defray expenses.

Because I lived in Missouri near the Truman Library during my sabbatical year, my fiancée, Kathryn Walker, whose own teaching career required that she remain in Arizona, endured with me long periods of separation. Throughout it all, hers was an unwavering, much appreciated voice of encouragement.

M. M. P.

Flagstaff, Arizona
November 25, 1981

STRICTLY PERSONAL AND CONFIDENTIAL
The Letters Harry Truman Never Mailed

Chapter 1

HARRY TRUMAN,
LETTER WRITER

The President of the United States showed his appointment secretary a copy of a letter he had penned that morning to a music critic. "You're not going to send this," the shocked aide asked Harry Truman. "It's already been mailed," he snapped. A few hours before, Margaret Truman's father had personally mailed Washington *Post* music critic Paul Hume the original letter, threatening to blacken Hume's eyes, calling him worse than a guttersnipe for his "lousy" review printed that morning of Margaret's current Washington, D.C., singing engagement. "You don't like that?" the President asked his stunned assistant. "Hell no!" he answered. "Wait a minute," Truman said, as he reached into his desk for another letter. "Here's the first draft." Dazed and defeated, the assistant sighed. "All right, I'll settle for the one you mailed."

As this volume reveals, Harry Truman, from the time he became President in 1945 until a few years before his death in 1972, wrote over one hundred and forty letters (a few of them wires and memos) that were not sent to the intended recipients. Included is a letter Truman wrote to Hume's boss asking him to *fire* the music critic! In other unmailed missives, he blasts a U.S. Supreme Court Justice for "that crazy decision that has tied up the country"; calls noted Kansas City cultural benefactor William Rockhill Nelson "pigfaced," judging Nelson's character to be "lower than the belly of a snake"; defends the firing of "God's right hand man," General Douglas MacArthur; describes Richard Nixon as a "squirrel head"; and labels two Democratic representatives from his hometown's congressional district "double barrelled shit asses."

But not all of the unmailed correspondence presented here are "spasms" or "mad letters" — Truman's own names for his angry, impulsive, shoot-from-the-hip responses. A number find the President writing candidly, usually too candidly for the moment, about such things as why he directed use of atomic bombs against Japan, his assessment of world leaders and international affairs, his joys and frustrations over running the government, his reflections on history (including the sadness he felt at President John F. Kennedy's funeral), as well as his devotion to his family, neighbors, and country.

"Just study the papers. You'll find what you need. All my papers are right here in the Library," Mr. Truman told me with a final thrust of his hand as I left his office in 1961. I had come during my Christmas break to the Truman Library in Independence, Missouri, as a graduate history student at the University of Missouri to research materials for a seminar assignment. Being able to ask a former President of the United States questions about the history he had helped make was an unexpected bonus.

It was actually our second meeting. My first introduction to Truman had taken place during a near blizzard a few days before when I had helped a janitor at the Truman Library push Mr. Truman's car out of a snowbank. He was driving by himself, and we watched him fishtail off the snow-packed street behind the Library when he tried to navigate a corner on his way home, situated about a half mile away.

"Now Mr. President, let up on the gas a little more! O.K. Mr. President, now put it in reverse," the janitor instructed the cheerful man behind the wheel, who so recently had been the world's most powerful leader. We worked together as a team that day — Harry Truman shifting gears, a yelling janitor and an excited college student pushing and shoving from behind — and we freed that car in short order. As I watched his green Chrysler disappear through the blowing snow, I thought, "What a man! Here he is, a former President of the United States, in his seventies, and he gets behind the wheel and ventures out by himself on a day like this!"[1]

After that, my research trips to the Truman Library became numerous and routine, first to study the President's papers for a doctoral dissertation about the Truman Administration's ill-fated promotion of a controversial national health-insurance plan, and then to expand the dissertation into a book. More recently, I began trekking back to the Library in between teaching duties at Northern Arizona University to research a biography covering the Truman "retirement" years. From watching him hold forth around his library in the early sixties, I knew, of course, that he hadn't really retired after he left Washington. For more than a decade afterward, he participated vigorously in local and national affairs. As a result, his post-presidential papers at the Library are massive, with his post-presidential correspondence alone requiring 220 linear feet of archival shelf space.

As I began to sort through that correspondence, I noticed the former Chief Executive's penchant for writing letters and not mailing them, and I told Library research archivist Erwin J. Mueller, "the *real* Harry Truman certainly comes through in these letters marked 'hold' or 'not sent.' " The

---

[1] I learned later that Mike Westwood, local Independence police officer, normally accompanied the former President on his outings.

deeper I probed, the more unmailed letters I found. Finally, torn between interest in HST's later years and fascination with these explicit letters, I wondered aloud to Mueller if the Truman White House files might also contain a lot of unmailed correspondence. Next morning, Mueller rolled a cart laden with boxes to my research-room table, each box filled with fat correspondence folders from those earlier White House days. By noontime I knew that the biography would have to wait. I found dozens of unmailed presidential letters addressed to a wide assortment of people and covering a broad spectrum of topics.

The files Mueller brought to me that day had been closed to scholars until recently, and they yielded ultimately two-thirds of the letters printed in this book. Called the "President's Secretary's Files" (PSF for short), they had been sequestered in an office at the Library used by HST's faithful, efficient, and *close-mouthed* personal secretary, Rose Conway. I had heard about these "secret" papers, withheld from the other Truman materials at the Library, during my graduate school days, and I remember how, over Saturday night pitchers of beer, we neophyte Truman scholars had grumbled about Mr. Truman's refusal to give historians access to them. Not until almost twenty years later, after looking at those papers and finding among them a torn manila folder labeled in Truman's hand "Strictly Personal & Confidential," did I appreciate the President's unwillingness to have them opened during his lifetime.

The remaining unmailed correspondence was scattered mostly through the Truman post-presidential materials. Like the PSF, until the late seventies these manuscripts had reposed in the former President's private wing of the Library, which had been sealed off following his death the day after Christmas in 1972. Actually, Mr. Truman had not used his Library office during the last six years of his life. So his desk, gathering dust, remained undisturbed for over a decade until

Library staff members Elizabeth Safly and Mildred Carol entered his private suite in early 1977 to inventory its contents. They found the drawers crammed with handwritten memos, essays, unmailed letters, and layer upon layer of other assorted accumulation. Included were pictures, political badges, and medallions; awards, an arm band, and miniature cap gun; watches, tie clasps, and key chains; pocket knives, saved string, and postage stamps; Bibles, playing cards, and a long, narrow scratch pad printed across the top FOR NARROW MINDED PEOPLE — COMPLIMENTS HARRY S. TRUMAN.

Judging from the handwritten material found in his desk, Harry Truman himself could get mighty narrow-minded at times. When something got his "Missouri up," he vented anger by writing either a vituperative essay on the subject or a hot letter, like the one he sent to that music critic. Unlike that earlier famous "spasm," once his pulse rate had slowed to normal, these letters and essays had been shoved into a desk drawer and forgotten.[2]

Most of Truman's unmailed letters were typed, however, and usually by Miss Conway, who, for twenty-seven years commencing in 1945, had handled his personal correspondence. Roused to anger, HST often started dictating to Miss Conway a letter with even-tempered aplomb, but yielded halfway through to an emotional disregard for political niceties. Sometimes the President caught himself, broke off the dictation, and made a decision later on whether the typed-up draft with alteration could be mailed. Often it could not. If it was salvageable, the original draft went into Miss Conway's file cabinet. Of course, completed letters were also pigeonholed. This happened when the President, out of a sense of recovered equanimity (prodded into conscious-

---

[2]   Unhappily, however, the first unmailed draft of the letter sent to music critic Paul Hume was not found.

ness at times by a gentle word from Miss Conway, or a less gentle one from an adviser), instructed that the letter be held when it came back for his signature.

The remarkable thing is that Harry Truman saved all of these letters. Instead of jotting "destroy it" or "deep-six it" on a sensitive document, he wrote "file it." He did so because he insisted that the only *good* history was history based on "all the facts." To provide those facts upon which he would be judged, he started keeping personal notes when he entered politics in 1922, and saved nearly every scrap of paper, including his car's repair records, from the time he ran for the U.S. Senate in 1934. "A letter or memo considered by the President himself to be of no value may turn out to be the answer to historians to a vital question or decision . . ." he explained to a college group in 1954. "You know," he later wrote his close friend, former Secretary of State Dean Acheson, "I'm no scholar in any line — but I do know that our history and the men who made it have been left in the lurch. . . . That is the reason I'm so interested in having all the facts as we know them available. Maybe I am a nut on the subject. If I am I hope you'll bear with me."

Had Harry Truman not been "a nut on the subject," the unmailed letters in this volume would have been destroyed. Had his daughter, Margaret Truman Daniel, not shared her father's faith that the more people knew about his public service the better, these documents would have been screened and held from use by a committee or a family member — as is the case today at several presidential libraries — or worse, sealed for generations to come. Rather, we are privileged to become better acquainted through these pages with a man who, while not a college graduate, read biography and history extensively, who defended, perhaps too vigorously, any imagined insult to family and associates past and present, and who throughout it all displayed a zest for living, a great sense of humor, and a tremendous love of country.

Chapter 2

THE PRESS

The following longhand note, which Harry Truman penned sometime in the nineteen fifties, was found in his desk after his death.

"The Columnists & The Publishers"

The men who write columns for the classified press sell their writing ability just as the light-(lite?)-of-love ladies sell their bodies to the madam of a bawdy house. They write columns on policy in domestic affairs and on foreign affairs from the rumor source, and as long as the "madam" — the publisher, will pay them for this sort of bawdy thing, that's what they want.

In many cases, the publisher only wants talent to present his distorted viewpoint. Hearst, Pulitzer, Scripps-Howard, Gannett, Bertie McCormick and the Patterson chain are shining examples. Many a great and talented scribbler has sold his soul to these purveyors of "Character Assassination." The old Moslem assassins of Mesopotamia have a much better chance of a considered "judgment" in the end, than have these paid mental whores of the controller of our so-called "free press." This so-called "free press" is about as free as Stalin's press. The only difference is that Stalin frankly controlled his, and the publishers and owners of our press are always yapping about the Constitution and suppressing a free press.

News should never be edited. Editorials should be frankly the opinions of the owners and publishers, and should be so stated. But news should be reported as it happened.

I know of only one paper with a national circulation that prints all the news fit to print, and confines editorial opinion to the pages where it belongs.[1]

The Hearst, Knight, Pulitzer, McCormick-Patterson, L. A. Times, Dallas News, N. O. Times Picayune, are the worst news editors in the business — but I'm happy to say their thinking readers are aware of their mishandling of the facts, and their political influence is not what they'd like to have it.

Most public figures have trouble with the press. Harry Truman thought he was the target of a publishing conspiracy. He got "give-'em-hell mad" when he read what he called downright lies about himself and his family. And because he read so much (by age fifteen Harry had read nearly every book in the Independence Public Library), and because he figured most big newspapers and magazines were owned by the "high hats" who lined up behind the Republican Party, he found "lies" everywhere. There were lies about his early life, about his presidential programs, certainly about his chances to beat Republican Thomas E. Dewey for election in 1948. He had never been, after all, a member of the Establishment. Before entering politics, he had been a railroad timekeeper, bank clerk, Missouri dirt farmer, World War I artilleryman, and a Kansas City shopkeeper who went broke

---

[1] New York *Times.*

trying to sell men's clothing during "that Republican depression of 1921." Surely, Truman assumed, such a man couldn't get a fair shake from big-city millionaire publishers and their paid columnists and headline hunters. They were, he charged, the "opposition" or "kept press." "If [Pulitzer] and his ilk are in heaven I want to go to hell!" Truman wrote his cousin.

During his second year as President, Truman decided, in order to compete better with the communists on a global scale, to promote a State Department–directed Voice of America program. But while Congress debated his idea to beam radio broadcasts abroad, Associated Press director Kent Cooper spoke out against Truman's information program. The government had no business promoting "propaganda," Cooper wrote the President. In a speech, the AP chief argued that the country's private news services were doing an outstanding job in presenting America's case before the world.

Truman, just returned from a visit to his ailing ninety-four-year-old mother in Grandview, Missouri, drafted the first of many unmailed letters he wrote to journalists to be found scattered throughout his personal papers decades later.

[Early June 1947]

My dear Mr. Cooper:

I appreciated very much your letter of the twenty-third which reached me in Grandview about the twenty-sixth or twenty-seventh.

I am not a propaganda artist and don't believe in it but I do think there ought to be some way for the facts to be gotten to the people of the rest of the world, and these facts ought to be arranged so as to offset the propaganda of the opposition. Nothing ever takes place in Russia whether it is sending millions to concentration camps or chasing the Gov-

ernment of Hungary out of the country[2] but it is used to show
how good the Russians are. Unless we can offset that sort of
situation the crack pots will have us before we know it.

It seems to me that you, and the rest of the people who are
interested in the honest distribution of the news, ought to
work out some way with the State Department so our side
of the case can be put before the world. The things that are
put out as our side of the case are the worst propaganda in
the world. I lay that to some nutty radio commentators and
to our sabotage press.

There is no incentive for the distribution of information
behind the iron curtain. So who is to make that distribution
but the United States Government. If you have a better answer give it to me.

*A few weeks later, the President came across what he
considered a good example of poor journalism in the Richmond, Virginia,* Times-Dispatch. *The newspaper had told its
readers that President Truman and his traveling party had
just driven down one of their highways at reckless and un-
lawful speed. It didn't take Truman long to draft a rejoinder,
but he never sent it to the* Times-Dispatch.

                                                July 9, 1947
Gentlemen:

In your issue yesterday, you go out of your way to inform
your readers that the President of the United States exceeded
the safety speed limit in the drive from Monticello to Washington. That is not a true statement. I certainly did not expect
a great Virginia Daily to misrepresent the President of the
United States, willfully, when he was a guest of that great
State.

---

[2]   A Communist coup had just occurred in Hungary.

Here are the facts if you are interested in *facts*.

Arrangements were made to leave Colle, the home of Hon. Stanley Woodward,[3] where I stayed for my Virginia visit, which is just south of Monticello, at 8:15 A.M., so as to avoid the heavy Sunday traffic. We left Colle exactly on time. I was driving because I like to drive, and very seldom get a chance to drive. The Chief of Staff to the President, Adm. Leahy, the Secretary of the Treasury, Mr. Snyder, and General Graham, the White House physician, were passengers in the car.

The pace was set by a capable, efficient State Policeman, in a State Police car. His instructions were to obey every regulation — and he did just that. I could not have exceeded the Virginia speed law if I had desired to do so — which I did not.

A true story — the only one I saw in all the press — appeared in the New York Times. Yet the Times wrote almost as misleading an editorial as did your paper. I'm sorry in both instances.

The only reason I write you is that for more than twenty-five years I've been working for road safety. I've driven a car more than a million miles — and have never been charged with a traffic violation. I am doing all I can to stop what amounts to murder on the road.

Yet to put a kick in an editorial you use a wrong premise, to put it mildly.

I thought, perhaps, you might be interested in the facts.

When, at the start of his second term in 1949, the New York Times *editorialized that Truman's administration was "not distinguished for the excellence of its appointments," the President sent* Times *publisher Arthur Sulzberger a*

---

[3] Chief of Protocol, appointed later U.S. Ambassador to Canada.

memo in which he called the Times *story a "lousy lie." Because Sulzberger was in Europe,* Times *vice-president and general manager Julius Ochs Adler opened HST's letter and replied diplomatically, defending his newspaper's right to express its "considered opinion."*

The President scratched his never-to-be-mailed reaction on the back of Adler's letter.

May 15, 1949[4]

Your reply to my comment on your editorial on the appointment of a Secretary of the Army is most interesting.

Your "considered opinion" seems to be consistent with your "considered opinion" of last September and just about as reliable.

The previous September, the New York Times *had not been alone in forecasting Harry Truman's probable defeat in the upcoming November presidential election. Political pundits across the nation, backed by public-opinion polls conducted by Elmo Roper and others, predicted certain victory for Truman's Republican opponent, New York Governor, Thomas E. Dewey. Early election eve, Colonel Robert R. McCormick's conservative Chicago* Tribune, *wanting and expecting a Truman defeat, rushed an edition onto the streets bearing the headline* DEWEY DEFEATS TRUMAN. *But, when the final returns were in, Truman had won the most stunning upset in American political history. As HST explained in an unmailed letter to Roper afterward, he interpreted his win as a victory of the people over the press.*

---

[4]   Adler's letter was dated June 13. HST erred when he dated his reply *May 15.*

December 30, 1948

My dear Mr. Roper:

I have read with much interest your piece in this morning's Tribune headed "A Study of Election Results." It is interesting, but it still misses the main point. Candidates make election contests, not poll takers or press comments by paid column writers. Edited news columns and misleading headlines have some effect — not much. People in general have lost faith in the modern press and its policies.

That is a good thing, too. No one segment should be able to control public opinion. Leadership still counts. The publisher's press is a very small part of our population. They have debauched the responsibility they owe to the country and the people have shown them just how they like it.

Later the President wrote Roper again after receiving a conciliatory letter from the pollster. This time Truman mailed a reply, but one much shorter and far more diplomatic than this original draft.

September 22, 1951

Dear Mr. Roper:

I can't tell you how very much I appreciated your good letter of the twentieth. You referred to the 1948 campaign, and the only recollection I have is that a statement was made by a certain expert on political polls that a poll after September was not at all necessary because Dewey had the presidency in the bag. I had no ill feeling on account of that statement, but I had to go out and disprove it as best I could.

Your agreement on Dean Acheson highly pleases me because Dean is, I think, about the ablest Secretary of State we have had in several generations. He negotiated the Atlantic Pact which was a most difficult job, and succeeded in getting the Senate to agree to it. His performance at San

Francisco recently and at Ottawa are just samples of the way he does the number one job in the Cabinet of the President.

One of the difficult things of this day and age is the fact that some public men seem to have lost all idea of truth and moral responsibility. That, I think, has been brought about by the attitude of the publishers of certain newspapers. They employ men whose objective is to misrepresent public officials. This sort of newspaper salesmanship was inaugurated by Joseph Pulitzer who left a fund for awards to offset the terrible things he had done to people while he was alive. A great many people try to get right with God by leaving foundations. I don't think that has any effect on the Almighty.

The Hearst chain of newspapers is a shining example of the purchase of articles by character assassins.

The McCormick-Patterson chain is almost as bad, with the exception that they do their own character assassinations both in the news and editorials.

It has been my experience, and I have been in elective office about thirty years, that when people know the facts, these misrepresentations have no effect on them. I think that was very adequately proven in 1948.

I am sorry to have been so long-winded in answering your good letter, but sometime or other the American public is going to awake to the fact that what they want is news in an ungarbled form, and not the edited variety which we get most of the time these days.

Sincerely yours,

Truman's 1948 election dispelled the widely held belief that he could not have won the presidency in his own right, that he was an accident, an aberration in history, Franklin Roosevelt's errand boy who by chance inherited the great man's office. Reading his hometown newspaper one summer day in 1949, the thought struck Truman that old Bill South-

ern, publisher of the Independence Examiner, *must still believe that the present occupant of the White House was a nobody. Southern, who wrote a folksy column, "Solomon Wise," had sporadically opposed his neighbor Harry from the time Truman became a Jackson County administrator, or "Judge," as the position is known in Missouri.*

Southern never received this complaint from President Harry S. Truman.

July 8, 1949

Dear Mr. Southern:

Most days I read "Solomon Wise" in my hometown paper. I'm always disappointed when "Solomon" has hay fever or is otherwise incapacitated and his "column" doesn't appear.

Of course, there are days in a row when I do not receive the "hometown" paper, through no fault of anyone, but due to the fact that some 23,000 letters and as many circulars, advertising sheets and papers come to the White House *every day.*

I have a very efficient staff to look after the mail, but sometimes it is too much for the most efficient. Eighteen years ago, one man could take care of the White House mail. He assigned it to a half dozen people to answer. Now we have twenty-five to mark and assign it, besides a half dozen secretaries, and executive assistants, and four hundred helpers to answer it all. I myself sign my name six hundred times a day to documents, orders, and private mail.

When I was on the County Court, I signed my name six hundred times a day to orders, warrants and letters — so it is natural to me.

What I started out to say was that I see Less Byam, an indicted County Judge, mentioned in your ten and twenty year ago columns. I see Mel Pallette. I see numerous and sundry people most of whom I know — *some* favorably — but I never see any mention editorially, ten year, twenty year or thirty-five year ago, about a former resident of Independence, who was Eastern Judge for two years, Presiding Judge for eight years in Jackson County and ten years United States Senator from Missouri; also Vice President for *almost* three months, and then President for and elected to be President for a full term.

This no good fellow fooled you on the road fund expenditure, who fooled you on his first campaign for U.S. Senator, who fooled you for his second campaign for senator, and who really put you in the hole on his campaign for President of the United States — is and will be president for three and a half more years — come hell or high water — and maybe longer if he wants to be.

This is all true — yet his hometown editor — a grand old man I'd say — can't possibly admit that his hometown has a number one world citizen who *may* (?) be a credit to his hometown. I wonder why!

It makes no difference to me. I won both senatorial elections with all the press against me and a presidential election with ninety percent of them against me, all the pollsters, all the "ivory tower" columnists, the gamblers and everybody but the people against me.

And, I'll do it again if it becomes necessary. What I wonder about, is why my friend, my original backer and my hometown editor, acts like that old character assassin Joe Pulitzer or Bertie McCormick or William Randolph Hearst. Is it circulation, advertising or what? I think it's a what.

The Kansas City Star, *largest newspaper in Independence's big neighbor to the west, had opposed Truman consistently. Friendly support came only from smaller, less influential Kansas City newspapers, like Garrett Smalley's weekly* News-Press. *When Smalley visited Florida in the summer of 1949, he replied to a Miami* Herald *editorial attacking Truman. He sent the newspaper a letter defending HST but, as Smalley later explained to the President, he had included in his letter a compliment about the* Herald, *fearful that otherwise the newspaper wouldn't publish his rebuttal.*

Harry Truman drafted, then filed away, all but the first and last sentences of the reply sent to Smalley.

October 18, 1949

Dear Garrett:

I appreciated your letter of the 12th, enclosing a copy of a letter that you wrote to the Voice of the People in the Miami Herald.

If you don't know it, that's a Jack Knight paper, and runs Hearst and Roy Howard[5] a close second for being one of the rottenest publications in the country.

I suppose it was necessary for you to compliment them, in order to get your letter published, but I would much rather have them saying nasty things about me than good things.

When they commence saying good things about me, I'll know I'm wrong.

Sincerely yours,
Harry S. Truman

The glow Truman felt after his upset victory in 1948 was short-lived. Public concern over Russia's threat to world peace, and reports that a Soviet spy network operated within our government, heightened in 1949 after Chiang Kai-shek's Nationalist China fell to the Reds on China's mainland, and former State Department official Alger Hiss went on trial accused of having lied about once having been a Communist. By spring 1950, Truman had a full-scale Red Scare on his hands. Its leader was Wisconsin Republican United States Senator Joseph R. McCarthy, whose demagogic crusade to

---

5 Howard was president of Scripps-Howard newspapers and editor of the New York *World-Telegram.*

root out "pinks" from government continued into the first years of Eisenhower's presidency.

In 1954, after Truman retired to Independence, he received a bulky and hostile letter from Buffalo, New York, newspaper columnist Burt Drummond. Drummond enclosed clippings of columns he had written supporting the McCarthy claims that Truman, especially during his 1948 campaign, knowing full well that Communists existed in government, had denied it, calling such an accusation "a red herring." The evidence was overwhelming, Drummond told Truman, "that you alone, of all the Chief Executives of our nation, won the privilege of occupying the White House by resorting unashamedly to falsehood and fraud in its quest!" HST snapped off a "Don't mail. File it" retort.

May 26, 1954

Dear Mr. Drummond:

I have seen everything now. I know it has been customary for the Hearst papers, and to some extent the Scripps Howard, to publish misinformation on the front page and then write an editorial about it. But you are the first gutter columnist to write a letter, such as the one you wrote me.

I have always hoped that sometime or other, your type of columnist would reform and tell the truth. Maybe sometime you will.

While not endorsing the McCarthyite claim that Truman shielded Communists in government, the Washington Post *had in 1950 urged formation of a sweeping commission to investigate "the internal menace of the fifth column," along with our national defense posture. HST penned* Post *publisher Philip Graham his thoughts about the commission idea but withheld from the mail the bulk of his original broadside, which contained unrestrained jabs at the publishers and his political opposition.*

June 5, 1950

Dear Mr. Graham:

I read the editorial in your May twenty-second issue of the Washington Post with a great deal of interest, and I am inclined to think that there is an effort to set up a second Congress and Executive Department for the purpose of going around the elected representatives of the people. It is an interesting procedure.

It seems to me that if you newspaper men would sit down and analyze the situation for all it is worth, and then get behind the domestic and foreign program which this Administration advocates, we could accomplish something.

I can't see where the extra curricular Commission to which you refer would add anything to what we already know, and what we have already accomplished. I am not in favor of the government being operated by the Commission — if the elected officials of the government can't carry out their duties, support and defend the Constitution of the United States, then the people ought to elect men to the offices of responsibility who can do the job.

Understand, of course, that it was a most terrible disappointment to all the big guns of the press of the United States, when the people decided that they were satisfied with the present incumbent of the White House, and it has been the policy of a vast majority of the press ever since that election to do everything possible to discredit the policies which the people want implemented. I am sorry this is the case, but I suppose editors and publishers are human, just as are politicians.

We might seriously consider making Mr. Eugene Meyer[6] Chairman of a Commission consisting of Robert R. McCormick, William Randolph Hearst, Jr., Mr. J. W. Knight of the Chicago Daily News and Miami Herald, Mr. Roy

---

6   Washington *Post* owner.

Howard, little Napoleon of the United Press and the Scripps-Howard chain, and Roy Roberts, the managing editor of the Kansas City Star, along with Uncle Joe Pulitzer, the publisher of the St. Louis Post-Dispatch. It seems to me that these gentlemen might be able to settle all the difficulties of the world. They know how to tell those responsible what to do.

It might be worth a trial. We could appoint a committee consisting of Mr. McCormick, Mr. Hearst, and possibly Jesse Jones[7] to go to Moscow and have sub-committees go to England, France and even maybe go to Formosa. Probably Senator Knowland[8] would be the man to head the Formosa group with the publisher of the Cleveland Plain Dealer and the San Francisco Call-Bulletin as his coordinators. We probably would come out with a settlement that would be highly satisfactory to Chiang Kai-shek and Dr. Judd.[9]

As I say, I am very much intrigued with your wonderful dream and naturally as you can understand, I am trying to make a suggestion that will be constructive in carrying it out. But my views are contained in the second and third paragraphs of this letter.

Your country's future is at stake, just as it was in 1776, 1814, 1860 and 1917. Free press and free enterprise must assume responsibility if the future of the human race is to survive as you and I want it.

Sincerely yours,
Harry S. Truman

---

[7]   Texas financier who served as Roosevelt's Secretary of Commerce.

[8]   Republican William F. Knowland, from a newspaper family in Oakland, California, who became known as "China Bill" for his heated opposition to Truman in support of Formosa-bound deposed Chinese leader Chiang Kai-shek.

[9]   Walter Judd, Republican congressman from Minnesota, who had served as a medical missionary in China.

"Your country's future is at stake," the President wrote. Three weeks later North Korea attacked South Korea and those words were used in a different, more ominous, context. Soon the American people were at war, even though it was called officially "a United Nations police action." Truman's early determination to limit the war to Korea enraged the McCarthyites. It also triggered a heated debate in the press.

The Reporter *magazine sided with Harry Truman. In its August 15, 1950, issue,* The Reporter *applauded Truman's "budgeted" approach in Korea, arguing that the days were gone for "an all-out, once-and-for-all effort" like in World War II. The magazine also ran a lengthy story detailing how, in its judgment, the Henry Luce publications* Time *and* Life *were teaming up with the Hearst and McCormick newspaper chains to undermine the President's foreign policy.*

In an unmailed letter, Harry Truman expressed his appreciation to Douglas Cater, the publication's Washington bureau chief.

August 12, 1950

Dear Mr. Cater:

Charlie Ross handed me the August fifteenth copy of the Reporter, and I read with a lot of interest the first page of the Reporter's notes and the article on Henry Luce, as well as several of the other articles.

It is certainly a very great satisfaction to see that somebody who is interested in facts is editing the gentlemen like Henry Luce, Mr. McCormick and Mr. Hearst.

In going over newspaper reports of the administrations of Washington, Jefferson, John Quincy Adams, Andrew Jackson, Lincoln, Grover Cleveland and Woodrow Wilson, I find that in every one of those administrations there were Hearsts, McCormicks and Luces, so those gentlemen's distortion of facts and misrepresentation of motives as far as this administration is concerned have no effect on me. But, when I find that somebody has analyzed the situation and put it in words as well as you have done in this number of The Reporter, it pleases me highly. The only thing we should be careful about is that the history of this period shall be based on facts and not on fiction and prejudice.

Sincerely yours,
Harry S. Truman

In contrast, Frank Kent of the Washington Evening Star *became the target of Truman's wrath after Kent editorialized that the President could not hide his administration's "odoriferous" stench uncovered by recent investigations into alleged gift-taking by officials within his administration. Kent never got a chance to read Truman's critique of his exposé.*

September 2, 1951

My dear Mr. Kent:

I have read your latest spasm in the Washington Star of this morning. The prostitutes of the mind, in my opinion — and it is only one man's — are much more dangerous to the future welfare of mankind than the prostitutes of the body.

The top mind prostitutor was, of course, William Randolph Hearst. He was not only a top prostitute of the mind, he was the No. 1 whore monger of our time.

Did any of our top notch publications take notice of that fact?

I'm sorry to see you in your old age join these prostitutes of the mind of our great Republic. Your article today is rank prostitution in its worst form.

My suggestion to you is to read Matthew V, VI, VII and put your stones in your own pocket rather than throw them at your betters.

H.S.T.

Other newspaper columnists who especially irritated Truman included Fulton Louis, Jr., Drew Pearson, Westbrook Pegler, and Walter Winchell. The last two were subjects of unmailed letters after HST left the presidency. Requested to contribute something to a testimonial volume honoring Westbrook Pegler, Truman recorded this reaction.

October 2, 1954

Dear Mr. Greene:

I was very much surprised to learn that you plan to make an award to the greatest character assassin in the United States. I believe there is no one in the country, unless it is Fulton Lewis, who has done more harm to good people than the man you propose to honor.

It is difficult to understand, but perhaps it is your intention to place men of such caliber on a pedestal.

Sincerely yours,

Harry S. Truman

As for Walter Winchell, Harry had once written his sister Mary Jane that "if I could have gotten my hands on him, I'd have tried to break his neck!" The President's intense dislike of Winchell did not diminish with time. Asked to use his influence with a fraternal organization to persuade it to stop cooperating with the journalist, HST filed away his terse response.

[Late January 1956]

[Dear Mr. Holmes:]

Replying to your letter of January 27th, my suggestion to you is never to get into an argument with anyone of Winchell's caliber. You just give them further advertising. If Winchell ever told the truth it was by accident and not intentional.

Concern over America's internal security reached a peak in the early fifties after Russia exploded its first atom bomb in 1949. Like others, Truman feared that the Soviets had obtained U.S. military secrets, but unlike his critics, who claimed that spies worked within government, he blamed the nation's news media. In September 1951, HST issued an order tightening up government information releases. He claimed that 95 percent of our military secrets had been published, and in a press conference, he gave as an example Fortune *magazine, which he charged had printed the locations, and even maps, of our atomic-energy plants.*

But the published article that first alerted Truman to the security leak problem had appeared the previous summer in American Aviation *magazine, as seen from this unmailed complaint to that magazine's publisher.*

[Mid-July 1951]

Memo to Wayne W. Parrish:

From the President, U.S.A.:

The attached page[10] is most interesting — to the Kremlin.

I'd like very much to have the same information about the Soviets. Will you please publish that information? The C.I.A. doesn't seem to be able to get it.

Since you've given the Soviets our proposed strength and organization, maybe you can give me theirs. It would be highly appreciated.

H.S.T.

A few days after Truman called the press in to scold them about security leaks, New York Times *Washington correspondent Arthur Krock editorialized that the President was*

---

[10]   Only a tiny corner of the page remained stapled to the memo; the rest, cut away, was missing from the file.

wrong, that his advisers had misled him, that the press had not given out our military secrets. Truman put down his newspaper and took up his pen. His letter to Krock was found a quarter-century later amongst HST's personal hand-written notes.

October 7, 1951

My dear Arthur:

I've just read your column about my security press conference. You give me credit for the responsibility of the men who were the sources of the information about which I talked. I wish that were true.

You see, the Generals and the Admirals and the career men in government look upon the occupant of the White House as only a temporary nuisance who soon will be succeeded by another temporary occupant who won't find out what it is all about for a long time, and then it will be too late to do anything about it.

You newspaper men have a complex that anyone who tells you of any of your many shortcomings is either ambitious to be a dictator or else he is an ignoramus. But you should take into consideration that we are no longer in the gay nineties of Ben Harrison, William McKinley or Teddy the Rough Rider.

We are faced with the most terrible responsibility that any nation ever faced. From Darius I's Persia, Alexander's Greece, Hadrian's Rome, Victoria's Britain, no nation or group of nations has had our responsibilities. If we could spend one year's military appropriation to develop the Euphrates Valley, the plateau of Ethiopia, the tableland of South America — if we could open the Rhine-Danube waterway, the Kiel Canal, the Black Sea Straits to free trade, if Russia would be a good neighbor and use her military expenditures for her own economic development, I would not have to scold the publishers for giving away our military secrets. Wish you'd do a little soul searching and see if at *great* intervals, the President may be right.

The country is yours as well as mine. You find no trouble in suppressing news in which I'm interested. Why can't you do a little safety policing?

There were lighter moments in the President's relationship with the press. He especially enjoyed bantering with the photographers and with various members of the White House press corps. One of Truman's favorites was Tony Vaccaro of Associated Press.

Vaccaro, about to return to Washington with the other newsmen after covering a presidential stay in Key West, Florida, jokingly wrote Truman about some things he had learned during the trip: that Old Taylor bourbon didn't work as a suntan oil, that you couldn't win big at poker unless you brought your own deck of cards, that Press Secretary Charlie Ross always called meetings just when the beach seemed most inviting, and that he (Vaccaro) needed to sleep more outside of church.

The President answered Vaccaro when he got back to the White House, but then jotted a note to his secretary, Rose Conway — "Rose, file it. H.S.T."

April 12, 1950

Memorandum for: Tony Vaccaro
From: The President

Your message of the ninth was carefully noted. I am most happy to have the information that Old Taylor doesn't serve well as suntan oil.

Your suggestion about the possibility of a double win with your own deck, I think, has a lot of merit.

I have spoken to Mr. Ross about a change in time for Press Conferences.

That idea of sleeping more away from church services is a good one. I've come to the conclusion myself that church is a very handy place to have a nap in most instances.

H.S.T.

[*In hand*] Where were you today? This is not Key West.

And Truman also relished reading a New Yorker *"Talk of the Town" column during his last year as President. The magazine reported that it had just received a letter from a friend in St. Louis who had passed along a communication from the St. Louis–headquartered International Mark Twain Society. The society's letterhead was most impressive, said the* New Yorker, *with Harry Truman listed as honorary I.M.T.S. president, Herbert Hoover one of the honorary vice-presidents, and Winston Churchill chairman of its biographical committee.*

The President gave the New Yorker *the lowdown on the International Mark Twain Society but resisted the temptation to put his corrective in the mail.*

January 8, 1952

Dear New Yorker:

I've been reading your January 5 Talk of the Town — and you've been taken in by one of Missouri's lovable old fakers, Cyril Clemens — at one time there was a t before the s! He claims to be a seventh — it may be seventeenth — cousin of Hannibal's (Missouri not Carthage) well-known humorist, Mark.

He has carried on a copious, one way letter writing for his I.M.T.S. for years and years. How I wish my lamented friend and press secretary Charlie Ross, had lived to see you taken in!

He is the International Mark Twain Society, and he merely puts people into it with a "by-your-leave" or any other formula. You'll get in now and no doubt be the recipient of nutty letters like the enclosed — which is my latest.

I don't know him, never saw him and don't want to. But of all the things to happen — the New Yorker to be hooked. It is almost as bad as the Nobel Board being hooked by that other old Missouri lovable faker Ewing Cockrell,[11] son of Francis Marion Cockrell, a Senator from Missouri for thirty years. So you are in good company.

Mark, himself, was a kind of a charlatan and faker — but all natives of Missouri love him — he was the lying columnist of his day. We have lots of 'em now, but no Sam Clemenses.

This is a personal and confidential communication. You may publish it when I retire — which may be some time yet.

---

[11] Ewing Cockrell had written a number of tracts proposing methods to achieve world disarmament, and in 1944 had obtained a great number of signatures approving his "Declaration of Ten Fundamental Peace Policies." The President apparently considered them more humorous than serious.

Chapter 3

THE WAR,
THE A-BOMB,
& AFTER

Desk Note
[June 1946]

Call in [*CIO's*] Phil Murray, [*AFL's*] William Green, Carpenter's Hutcheson, Dan Tobin [*of*] Teamster's Union, [*UAW's*] R. J. Thomas, Longshoremen, Sidney Hillman, [*James Petrillo, the*] S.O.B. of Musicians, and some others. Tell them that patience is exhausted. Declare an emergency — call out the troops. Start industry and put anyone to work who wants to work. If any leader interferes, court-martial him. [*John L.*] Lewis ought to have been shot in 1942, but Franklin didn't have the guts to do it. . . . Adjourn Congress and run the country.

Get plenty of Atomic Bombs on hand — drop one on Stalin, put the United Nations to work and eventually set up a free world.

Battle plans of a latter-day Napoleon? No. These are an embattled American President's strictly personal and confidential musings, wishing whimsically he still had those wartime powers of a year before — power to enforce order at home and peace abroad. By dropping atom bombs on Japan, Harry Truman had swiftly ended a world war. Yet within months of V-J Day he was buffeted by domestic warfare and the disintegration of a wartime alliance with Russia. A million and a half American workers struck the steel, auto, electrical, and meat-packing industries. By springtime of 1946, other unions threatened strikes, especially John L. Lewis's coal miners and those who worked the nation's railroads. To abort a paralyzing rail stoppage, the President actually did ask Congress for authority to draft strikers into the Army. As for America's recent ally, Joseph Stalin, Truman agreed with Britain's Winston Churchill when he said in 1946 that Stalin, ignoring diplomatic pledges, had enslaved millions to a life of Communism behind an "iron curtain."

Truman had met Churchill and Stalin in mid-1945 at Potsdam, a village in Germany, to map out postwar arrangements in Europe and combined war strategy against the still undefeated Japanese. This Potsdam diplomatic conference became the subject of an unmailed Truman letter years later. HST's onetime Secretary of State, Dean Acheson, on behalf of Harvard historian Herbert Feis, telephoned Truman to ask that he see Feis, who was researching a book covering our wartime diplomacy and wanted to learn more about the Potsdam conference. Truman later informed Acheson. "I wrote you a longhand letter after I talked to you about the Potsdam papers but I haven't made up my mind to send it." He never did.

March 15, 1957

Dear Dean:

It was certainly a pleasure to talk with you about Potsdam and the Doctor who is interested in that phase of our foreign policy.

I hardly ever look back for the purpose of contemplating "what might have been." Potsdam brings to mind "what might have been" had you been there instead of the Congressman, Senator, Supreme Court Justice, Presidential Assistant, Secretary of State, Governor of Secession South Carolina, the Honorable James F. Byrnes!

At that time I trusted him implicitly — and he was then conniving to run the Presidency over my head! I had Joe Davies, at that time a Russophile as most of us were, Ed Pauley, the only hard boiled hard hitting anti-Russian around except the tough old Admiral, Bill Leahy. Certainly things were presented because Russia had no program except to take over the free part of Europe, kill as many Germans as possible and fool the Western Alliance. Britain only wanted to control the Eastern Mediterranean, keep India, oil in Persia, the Suez Canal and whatever else was floating loose.

There was an innocent idealist at one corner of that Round Table who wanted free waterways, Danube-Rhein-Kiel Canal, Suez, Black Sea Straits, Panama all free, a restoration of Germany, France, Italy, Poland, Czechoslovakia, Rumania and the Balkans and a proper treatment of Latvia, Lithuania, Finland, free Philippines, Indonesia, Indo China, a Chinese Republic and a free Japan.

What a show that was! But a large number of agreements were reached in spite of the setup — only to be broken as soon as the unconscionable Russian Dictator returned to Moscow! And I liked the little son of a bitch. He was a good six inches shorter than I am and even Churchill was only three inches taller than Joe![1] Yet I was the little man in stature and intellect! Well we'll see.

Wish you [*had*] been there. Tell your friend I'll help him all I can. My best to Alice.

---

[1]   Truman stood 5 feet 9 inches tall.

Herbert Feis interviewed Truman and published his book, which traced the final phases of World War II. For a projected scholarly article, Feis contacted Truman again, this time to ask that he pinpoint when he directed use of the atomic bomb on Hiroshima, and to detail just how that order was carried out. Feis's new inquiry found Truman in a far less cooperative mood. After writing his reply, HST jotted across Feis's letter, "Just file it with proposed answer which was never sent!"

[Late April 1962]

My dear Mr. Feis:

You write just like the usual egghead. The facts are before you but you'd like to garble them. The instruction of July 25th, 1945 was final. It was made by the Commander in Chief after Japan refused to surrender.

Churchill, Stimson,[2] Patterson,[3] Eisenhower and all the rest agreed that it had to be done. It was. It ended the Jap War. That was the objective. Now if you can think of any other, "if, as, and when" egghead contemplations, bring them out.

You get the same answer — to end the Jap War and save ¼ of a million of our youngsters and that many Japs from death and twice that many on each side from being maimed for life.

It is a great thing that you or any other contemplator "after the fact" didn't have to make the decision.

Our boys would all be dead.

Asked often during his later years, "Why did you use the atomic bomb?" Truman never backed down from his belief

---

[2]   Henry L. Stimson, Secretary of War.
[3]   Robert P. Patterson, who succeeded Stimson as Secretary of War.

that its use was necessary. When in 1958 the Hiroshima city council sent him a resolution deploring his televised statement that given similar conditions he would order the bomb's use again, the former President drafted a no-compromise response to the Hiroshima city fathers. "We'll send it air mail," he instructed Rose Conway. "Be sure enough stamps are on it!"

Rarely did Truman receive favorable comment on his wartime A-bomb decision. One did appear in a Chicago Sun Times *column by Irv Kupcinet in which Kup presented the President's side of the controversy. Pleased, HST dictated Kup a thank you, but, even though he assured Kup, "this letter is not confidential," he later told his secretary, "Hold this letter."*

August 5, 1963

Dear Kup:

I appreciated most highly your column of July 30th, a copy of which you sent me.

I have been rather careful not to comment on the articles that have been written on the dropping of the bomb for the simple reason that the dropping of the bomb was completely and thoroughly explained in my Memoirs, and it was done to save 125,000 youngsters on the American side and 125,000 on the Japanese side from getting killed and that is what it did. It probably also saved a half million youngsters on both sides from being maimed for life.

You must always remember that people forget, as you said in your column, that the bombing of Pearl Harbor was done while we were at peace with Japan and trying our best to negotiate a treaty with them.

All you have to do is to go out and stand on the keel of the Battleship in Pearl Harbor with the 3,000 youngsters underneath it who had no chance whatever of saving their lives. That is true of two or three other battleships that were sunk in Pearl Harbor. Altogether, there were between 3,000 and 6,000 youngsters killed at that time without any declaration of war. It was plain murder.

I knew what I was doing when I stopped the war that would have killed a half million youngsters on both sides if those bombs had not been dropped. I have no regrets and, under the same circumstances, I would do it again — and this letter is not confidential.

Sincerely yours,
Harry S. Truman

In Europe after the war, General Lucius D. Clay succeeded Dwight D. Eisenhower as military governor of American-occupied Germany. Clay, without consulting Truman, asked Johns-Manville Corporation chairman, Lewis H. Brown, to study and report on conditions there. Out of courtesy, Brown sent the President a copy of his completed report. In it, the businessman joined others who argued that Russian domination over East Germany and other eastern European regions could have been prevented had Roosevelt taken Churchill's advice. Churchill, with a wary eye on Stalin (as well as on British colonial interests), had urged in 1943 a joint U.S.-British thrust against Germany from the eastern Mediterranean. Instead, claimed Brown, U.S. commanders committed a "master mistake": they attacked Hitler through Italy and allowed the Russians an unobstructed highway into Central Europe.

Truman's unmailed reaction shows presidential anger, not only with Stalin's scrapping of pledges made at Potsdam, but with General Clay for not briefing the White House beforehand about Brown's study.

[August 30, 1947]

My dear Mr. Brown:

Thanks for your thoughtfulness in sending me a copy of your report on Germany. I'm just intrigued as to whom this report is addressed.

I notice you spent a great deal of time on the so-called Morgenthau plan[4] which never was considered at Potsdam at all and was in no way a part of the Potsdam agreement.

I was intrigued by your military strategy for the conquest of Yugoslavia and eastern Germany.

I was informed by the Chiefs of Staff that Churchill's plan for the invasion of Central Europe was a physical impossibility considering we had no bases anywhere in the Mediterranean at the time, but it is nice to speculate and comtemplate these things. In fact if we had held the line which we attained in Germany our troubles in that country with Russia would now be over but, of course, we did not know Russia was going to assume the attitude she has taken. Had the Potsdam Agreement been carried out we would be in no trouble in Germany, but we are faced with a condition and not a theory.

I appreciate the courtesy in sending me a copy of the report. Somebody you know has to implement these things from the beginning — I have always been under the impression that it was the President of the United States — maybe I am wrong.

Sincerely yours,

Truman would not tolerate being kept in the dark by subordinates. THE BUCK STOPS HERE, *read the sign on his desk, and he insisted upon immediate access to the facts he needed*

---

4   This plan, promoted by FDR's Treasury Secretary Henry J. Morgan-thau, Jr., would have transformed postwar Germany into a nonindustrial, agrarian state. Truman abhorred the idea.

to make final decisions. His first-named secretary of state, James Byrnes, discovered that in short order. Byrnes thought that Roosevelt had made a big mistake in 1944 by choosing Truman rather than him for Vice-President. Consequently, in running the State Department, Byrnes often acted as though he, not Truman, had the final say.

In late 1945, Byrnes attended a foreign minister's conference in Moscow and the President fumed over not hearing from him while he talked with the Russians. When Byrnes returned to Washington, according to Truman, Truman called the secretary into the oval office and read aloud a letter he had written him. In addition to dressing Byrnes down for keeping him in the dark, the letter gives an overview of the President's thinking about Russia at the time, and Truman later printed the letter in his memoirs. The original handwritten draft is now among Truman's presidential papers.

January 5, 1946

My dear Jim:

I have been considering some of our difficulties. As you know I would like to pursue a policy of delegating authority to the members of the cabinet in their various fields and then back them up in the results. But in doing that and in carrying out that policy I do not intend to turn over the complete authority of the President nor to forgo the President's prerogative to make the final decision.

Therefore it is absolutely necessary that the President should be kept fully informed on what is taking place. This is vitally necessary when negotiations are taking place in a foreign capital, or even in another city than Washington. This procedure is necessary in domestic affairs and it is vital in foreign affairs.

At San Francisco no agreements or compromises were ever agreed to without my approval. At London you were in constant touch with me and communication was established daily if necessary.

That procedure did not take place at this last conference. I only saw you for a possible thirty minutes the night before you left after your interview with the Senate Committee.

I received no communication from you directly while you were in Moscow. The only message I had from you came as a reply to one which I had Under Secretary Acheson send to you about my interview with the Senate Committee on Atomic Energy.

The protocol was not submitted to me, nor was the communiqué. I was completely in the dark on the whole conference until I requested you to come to the Williamsburg[5] and inform me. The communiqué was released before I even saw it.

Now I have the utmost confidence in you and in your ability but there should be a complete understanding between us on procedure. Hence this memorandum.

For the first time I read the Ethridge letter[6] this morning. It is full of information on Rumania & Bulgaria and confirms our previous information on those two police states. I am not going to agree to the recognition of those governments unless they are radically changed.

I think we ought to protest with all the vigor of which we are capable the Russian program in Iran. There is no justification for it. It is a parallel to the program of Russia in Latvia, Estonia and Lithuania. It is also in line with the high handed and the arbitrary manner in which Russia acted in Poland.

---

5   U.S.S. *Williamsburg,* the presidential yacht, where Truman first met with Byrnes upon his return.
6   A report submitted a month earlier to Secretary Byrnes at Byrnes' request by Kentucky journalist Mark Ethridge after Ethridge toured Soviet-dominated Rumania and Bulgaria.

At Potsdam we were faced with an accomplished fact and were, by circumstances, almost forced to agree to Russian occupation of Eastern Poland and the occupation of that part of Germany east of the Oder River by Poland. It was a high handed outrage.

At the time we were anxious for Russian entry into the Japanese War. Of course we found later that we didn't need Russia there and the Russians have been a head ache to us ever since.

When you went to Moscow you were faced with another accomplished fact in Iran. Another outrage if ever I saw one.

Iran was our ally in the war. Iran was Russia's ally in the war. Iran agreed to the free passage of arms, ammunition and other supplies running into millions of tons across her territory from the Persian Gulf to the Caspian Sea. Without these supplies, furnished by the United States, Russia would have been ignominiously defeated. Yet now Russia stirs up rebellion and keeps troops on the soil of her friend and ally, Iran.

There isn't a doubt in my mind that Russia intends an invasion of Turkey and the seizure of the Black Sea Straits to the Mediterranean. Unless Russia is faced with an iron fist and strong language another war is in the making. Only one language do they understand — "How many divisions have you?"

I do not think we should play compromise any longer. We should refuse to recognize Rumania and Bulgaria until they comply with our requirements; we should let our position on Iran be known in no uncertain terms and we should continue to insist on the internationalization of the Kiel Canal, the Rhine-Danube waterway and the Black Sea Straits and we should maintain complete control of Japan and the Pacific. We should rehabilitate China and create a strong central government there. We should do the same for Korea.

Then we should insist on the return of our ships from

Russia and force a settlement of the Lend-Lease Debt of Russia.

I'm tired babying the Soviets.

Truman didn't ask his Secretary of State to resign after their tiff; Byrnes's departure came later and voluntarily. But regardless of his private doubts about Byrnes, Truman boiled when he received a telegram from the United Farm Equipment and Metal Workers Union (CIO) demanding the secretary's resignation. The union, meeting in its annual session, charged that Byrnes's recent speech urging creation of a unified postwar German government flew in the face of our wartime sacrifice. The union also charged that Byrnes' earlier record as a United States senator had been one of hostility toward organized labor and minorities.

The President intended to respond, but then, despite an impulse to defend Byrnes, changed his mind. The letter to the union's president was not dispatched, probably because Truman knew that the Secretary of State would indeed be replaced in the not-too-distant future.

September 12, 1946

Dear Mr. Oakes:

I read your telegram of the tenth with a great deal of interest and outside of the fact there isn't a true statement in it, it is an interesting document.

As far as the Secretary of State is concerned, the President appoints a Secretary of State in whom he has confidence and that will continue to be the policy of this Administration. Mr. Byrnes will stay.

Sincerely yours,

Mr. Byrnes stayed on the job only a short while longer. During his tenure as Secretary of State, one of the most pressing concerns he and the President faced was instability in the Middle East. British power, so dominant in the Mediterranean before the war, had waned. Lest Russia move in, the United States took Britain's place. To contain communist expansion in the region in 1947, Truman reversed America's older isolationist tradition by successfully persuading Congress to provide funds to aid Communist-threatened Greece and Turkey (the Truman Doctrine). Later, other military and economic programs designed to contain Soviet expansion were established. Included were the North Atlantic Treaty Organization (NATO) and the Marshall Plan, named after Byrnes' successor, former Army Chief of Staff, General George C. Marshall.

After he left office, Truman complained that many countries, especially France, showed resentment rather than appreciation of U.S. military and economic assistance given them during his administration. He did not include Greece in that category, however, and he was touched deeply when in 1962 the King and Queen of the Hellenes sent him personalized holiday greetings. Truman wrote them a thank you, but, realizing afterward that it was a bit too folksy for royalty, opted instead to send a formal reply. He filed away this one:

January 3, 1963

Your Majesties:

You will never know how very much I appreciated your wishes for a Merry Christmas and a Happy New Year.

When a retired farmer is remembered by the King and Queen of great historical Greece, it certainly makes him feel as if he made a contribution. Your card will be framed and hung in my Library office to show that people do not forget.

Mrs. Truman joins me in best wishes to you for the New Year.

Sincerely yours,

During Truman's presidency, another major challenge in the Middle East had been coping with the thousands of European Jews fleeing to Palestine from horrid memories of Nazi terror. A Jewish homeland there had been promised decades earlier by the British; predictably this Zionist dream met with Arab hostility. Truman sympathized with the Zionists but took a wait-and-see approach to the Zionist claim to Palestine. He resisted pressure from American Jewish groups who petitioned him to endorse the Zionist cause. Responding to one such appeal, Truman wrote to U.S. Senator Joseph H. Ball of Minnesota with characteristic off-the-cuff straightforwardness. Political and diplomatic prudence kept him from mailing the letter.

November 24, 1945

Dear Joe:

I appreciate your letter of the nineteenth and the quotation from the Palestine Histadruth Committee of Minneapolis.

I told the Jews that if they were willing to furnish me with five hundred thousand men to carry on a war with the Arabs, we could do what they are suggesting in the Resolution — otherwise we will have to negotiate awhile.

It is a very explosive situation we are facing and naturally I regret it very much but I don't think that you, or any of the other Senators, would be inclined to send a half dozen Divisions to Palestine to maintain a Jewish State.

What I am trying to do is to make the whole world safe for the Jews. Therefore, I don't feel like going to war for Palestine.

Sincerely yours,

Israel became a reality in May 1948 under United Nations auspices. Truman granted it de facto recognition eleven minutes after the Israelis proclaimed themselves a nation.

Another nation-state the President decided to recognize was the Vatican. Against the advice of Dean Acheson, who had replaced Marshall as Secretary of State, Truman took the controversial plunge in October 1951 and requested Senate ratification of General Mark W. Clark as first U.S. Ambassador to Vatican City. Congressional reaction was immediate and hostile; Clark quickly asked that his name be withdrawn. Meanwhile, the beleaguered President vented his anger in an unmailed rejoinder to insurance executive Irvin H. Harlamert, who had petitioned him against the appointment.

January 3, 1952

Dear Mr. Harlamert:

I read your note of December thirty-first with a great deal of interest and it seems to me that you have an entirely wrong approach to the idea of an Ambassador to Vatican City, which is an independent state in its own right.

There are Ambassadors there from nearly every country in the world, including a great many of the Satellite Countries behind the Iron Curtain. All the Moslem Countries are represented there and we should have a representative present there all the time, who can talk to these people and get us information which we cannot otherwise get.

The people who have been screaming about the appointment of an Ambassador to the Vatican are violently bigoted in their approach. It is just too bad. I hope you will do a little thinking on the subject and maybe you will come to a different conclusion.

Sincerely yours,

Torn between political and religious factions during Truman's era, as in more recent times, Iran posed an additional headache. The Russians finally withdrew, having occupied northern Iran during the war, but throughout his presidency

Truman feared that the Soviets might use any pretext to re-occupy their oil-rich neighbor. Things got especially touchy in 1951 when Iran, determined to nationalize her oil, clashed with the British, who refused to yield longtime claims to the Iranian oil fields. The United Nations debated the dispute, but an impasse developed amid rumors that Iran, along with Egypt, was embracing the Soviet Union in order to obtain Russia's support for her nationalistic claims.

Democratic Congressman George H. Fallon wrote the White House that this news disturbed him greatly, that while Iran and Egypt drifted toward the Soviet orbit, the United States, after spending billions to help them, stood by, be-trayed and seemingly powerless. Truman tucked away his answer to Fallon.

November 13, 1951

Dear Congressman Fallon:

I read your letter of the 7th with a great deal of interest. It is difficult to understand a viewpoint that becomes de-featist when there's a good chance of winning the peace.

The world has always been in turmoil. If you read the history of peace you'll find that there was never a time when there was not extreme danger of war with some foreign power. Since 1939, we've had a foreign policy, and since 1945, we've had a military policy. The two are necessary if we expect to maintain our place, and contribute to the peace of the world.

It is easy enough to just sit back and throw bricks at the man who has to make decisions. It would be very much better to contribute a little cooperation. I hope you will think the thing through and decide to do just that.

Sincerely yours,

About the time Britain and Iran began clashing over oil, Henry F. Grady, who as U.S. Ambassador to Greece had distributed American aid sent there under the Truman Doctrine, moved from Athens to Tehran. Grady retired from the diplomatic corps before the British-Iranian dispute was resolved (it continued into the Eisenhower presidency). Piqued at his former boss, Dean Acheson,[7] Grady composed a Saturday Evening Post story. In "Headaches of an Ambassador," Grady veiled his reminiscences in humor, but the article dripped with caustic comment. He warned that rich Americans who gave fat presidential campaign donations hoping to be named as United States ambassadors, should expect headaches galore should their dream come true. The retired diplomat also poked fun at Secretary Acheson and others in the State Department, blaming failure to end the British-Iranian imbroglio upon Washington's habit of listening more to London than to America's man in Tehran — namely, him.

The President sent Grady a blistering retort. "My dear Henry. Or should I say Dr. Grady?" he began sarcastically. The Post article was "a sop to his ego," Truman accused, reminding Grady that "I have appointed more career diplomats to top places than all the Presidents together — and fewer 'fat cats' than any other President." HST defended Secretary Acheson, predicting, "Dean will be treated by history as our greatest Secretary of State. . . . But," concluded the President, "a man has to have a kick in the form of a personal attack if he sells an article to any of the dirty, slick, postal-subsidized magazines, and I understand."

Wounded, Henry Grady wrote the President that he had meant no offense by his article; that he realized that he had "apparently made a poor job of being humorous!" However, Grady did not agree with the President's "enthusiasm" for Dean Acheson. The problem in Iran, Grady insisted, was

---

[7]   Grady claimed that Acheson had reneged on a promise that he would be assigned as America's first postwar ambassador to Japan.

largely Acheson's fault, as well as the fault of obstinate British refusal to compromise.

Truman responded in hand to Grady, using words a bit different from this draft, which was discovered among his notes over a quarter century later.

Nov. 27, '52

Dear Henry:

I'll never call you Doctor again. Your reply to my spasm of a few days ago took all the fire out of me. I am very glad because in my book you are a great man.

Let me tell you something about the Iranian situation from this end: We held Cabinet meetings on it — we held Security Council meetings on it; and Dean, Bob Lovett,[8] Charlie Sawyer,[9] Harriman[10] and all the senior staff of Central Intelligence discussed that awful situation with me time and again.

The decisions were made by me, not by Dean. So, I'm to blame if things went hay wire. We tried two years before the final event to get the block headed British to have their oil company make a fair deal with Iran. No. They could not do that. They knew all about how to handle it — we didn't according to them.

We had Israel, Egypt, near east defense, Sudan, South Africa, Tunisia, the NATO treaties all on the fire. Britain and the Commonwealth Nations were and are absolutely essential if these things are successful. Then on top of it all we have Korea and Indo China. Iran was only one incident. Of course the man on the ground in each one of these places can only see his own problem. The President must see the whole picture and make his decisions accordingly. Maybe I

---

8   Robert A. Lovett, Secretary of Defense.
9   Charles Sawyer, Secretary of Commerce.
10 W. Averell Harriman, former U.S. Ambassador to Russia and Great Britain, then serving as the President's special assistant.

made some wrong ones — but I made them and I shall never run out on the men who carried them out.

Some day, when I leave this Great White Jail, I want to sit with you and discuss history from 1920 to 1953. We can have a great time!

Harry S. Truman

Chapter 4

STOPPING REDS
IN ASIA

Desk Note
June 30, 1950

Frank Pace[1] called at 5 A.M. E.D.T. I was already up and shaved. Said MacArthur wanted two divisions of ground troops. Authorized a regiment to be used in addition to the authorizations of yesterday, to be used at Mac's discretion.

Was briefed by Col Acoff[2] at seven o'clock. Called Pace and Louis Johnson[3] and told them to consider giving Mac-Arthur the two divisions he asked for and also to consider the advisability of accepting the two divisions offered by the Chinese Nationalist Government. That gov't is still recognized as the 5th permanent member of the Security Council U.N. Since Britain, Australia, Canada and the Netherlands have come in with ships and planes we probably should use the Chinese ground forces.

What will that do to Mao Tse-tung we don't know. Must

---

[1] Secretary of the Army.
[2] A Pentagon liaison officer.
[3] Secretary of Defense.

be careful not to cause a general Asiatic war. Russia is figuring on an attack in the Black Sea and toward the Persian Gulf. Both prizes Moscow has wanted since Ivan the Terrible who is now their hero with Stalin & Lenin.

Harry Truman had gone home to Independence for a rest that June weekend in 1950 when the Russian-backed North Korean army knifed across the 38th parallel in a surprise attack upon South Korea. "I'm so tired, I can hardly wait to get into the house," the President had confided to Bob Weatherford, his hometown's mayor, as they posed for photographers in front of Truman's big Victorian house. Word of the North Korean assault reached Independence that evening, eleven hours after the President had arrived. Next day, a still tired Harry Truman flew back to Washington.

Truman considered the North Korean attack another Soviet test of America's will to defend a remote and seemingly unimportant area of the world. Two years earlier, the Russians had blockaded West Berlin, and Truman, without resorting to war, retained access to the city by airlifting supplies to the encircled Berliners. Furthermore, the last thing Truman wanted was a war in Asia. Neither did our allies; Britain and France were just recovering economically from World War II. The United States and her friends would fight for South Korea, but in a limited way, in "a United Nations police action."

The chief danger, as Truman saw it, was being drawn into a war with Korea's neighbor, Communist China, and possibly even with the Soviet Union, which also bordered Korea. On Formosa, Chiang Kai-shek, chased off mainland China the year before, itched to return. After initial vacillation, Truman declined Chiang's offer of 33,000 troops for use in Korea, in order to prevent Chiang from maneuvering America into a massive war with Mao Tse-tung's China.

Chiang enjoyed powerful support in the United States (the President called it "the China Lobby"). A few days before the Korean War began, the White House had received a letter from Republican U.S. Representative Robert Hale, signed by a bipartisan group of other congressmen, urging the President to use every influence in the United Nations to prevent Chiang's removal from that world body. In the whirl of decision-making following outbreak of hostilities in Korea, Truman's dictated reply to Congressman Hale was never mailed.

June 28, 1950

Dear Congressman Hale:

I read your letter of the twenty-first with a great deal of interest and appreciate very much your suggestions regarding what the United Nations should do.

I have an idea that the United Nations General Assembly and Security Council work on the procedure followed by the Congress of the United States and I am sure that they have suggestions from all over the world about how they should transact their business just as you have the same sort of suggestions from all parts of your great State of Maine on how to run the Government of the United States.

Your suggestions will, of course, be passed along to our representatives in the United Nations and I am sure that every effort will be made to treat [*the*] Chinese fairly in that great organization.

Sincerely yours,

"Unleash Chiang Kai-shek!" Truman's opponents cried, especially when the Korean battles turned against the U.N. forces after Red Chinese "volunteers" joined the almost-defeated North Korean army. By late 1950, Americans and their U.N. allies were forced into bloody retreat. Robert

Earnest, a nineteen-year-old soldier from Dayton, Ohio, died during that retreat, and his grief-stricken mother wrote the President begging him to send more help to the boys fighting there. She also wanted him to find out if U.N. Commander General Douglas MacArthur and his staff knew what they were doing. She still had one surviving son in Korea, Mrs. Earnest said, and she explained that at his urging she had just painfully agreed to sign a waiver allowing him to enter combat.

The President received hundreds of letters from those whose loved ones fought in Korea, but his staff singled out Mrs. Earnest's and a reply was drafted. Truman later instructed, "Rose, file it. Do not mail."

February 8, 1951

My dear Mrs. Earnest:

I have your letter of January fourth and wish to extend to you my heartfelt sympathy in the loss of your youngest son, Robert.

I was deeply moved by your patriotic devotion in signing a waiver to permit your only remaining son to serve in the Navy without restrictions. I know what a sacrifice such a decision entailed.

With regard to General MacArthur and General Ridgway, you may rest assured that these outstanding officers are ever mindful of their great responsibilities and they have my complete confidence.

Again, let me express admiration of your fine spirit and courage.

Sincerely yours,

The President wasn't insensitive to such appeals. Mrs. Earnest's letter was held because by February 1951 Harry Truman could not honestly say that he believed General MacArthur to be "ever mindful" of his responsibilities or that MacArthur enjoyed his "complete confidence." The previous fall, Truman had conferred with the general on Wake Island while U.N. forces still held the upper hand in Korea, and when Truman asked him the likelihood of China's intervention should we march above the 38th parallel, MacArthur replied that chances of that happening were remote. But the Red Chinese did intervene. As their "volunteers" poured across the Yalu River out of Manchuria by the hundreds of thousands that winter, MacArthur urged the bombing of river bridges and selected Chinese targets.

Truman refused. He maintained that Europe, not Asia, was our first line of defense against communism; Russia, not China, our chief concern. He did not, as he reflected later, want to be "sucked into a bottomless pit" in Asia. The President would not yield.

Neither would Douglas MacArthur. Over the course of more than fifty years' military service, the general had come to believe that when forced to war, America did not pull its punches; that in wartime, politicians defer to military leadership, whose objective is the enemy's quick destruction.

Bewildered by political directives limiting his options in Korea, the general talked to the press, hinting that his troubles there stemmed from Washington's stupidity.

And MacArthur had a lot of company. "My son died for no reason at all," Mrs. Earnest had written the President. Why, she asked, don't we use the atom bomb? On Capitol Hill, Republicans especially questioned Truman's handling of the war. Representative Joseph Martin led opposition in the House, and in April 1951 Martin made public a letter he had received from General MacArthur. MacArthur told Martin that we should "follow the conventional pattern of meeting force with maximum counter-force. . . . There is no substitute for victory."

Harry Truman fired the general five days later. Public reaction was violently anti-Truman. People booed him at the

*Washington Senators opening baseball game, and in cities
across the land he and Secretary of State Acheson were
burned in effigy. Although former President Herbert Hoover
was generally friendly toward Truman, he urged MacArthur
to fly home quickly to take advantage of the mood. The
general returned triumphantly and addressed a joint session
of Congress, and talk filled the air about MacArthur becoming the Republican party's next presidential candidate.*

*Onetime boy-wonder Minnesota governor Harold E.
Stassen (who wanted that Republican presidential nomination himself) urged Truman to make up with the general,
cautioning him that if the rift between them were allowed to
run its bitter course, "it [could] do no good for our country."*

However benign, Truman withheld his reply to Stassen.

April 30, 1951

Dear Governor:

I read your letter of the twenty-eighth with a great deal of
interest and I more than appreciate your effort to help meet
a situation which is not a necessary one, I am sorry to say.

Thanks again for your interest in the matter.

Sincerely yours,

*Neither MacArthur nor Stassen won the Republican presi-
dential nomination in 1952; the GOP chose instead another
Army general, Dwight D. Eisenhower. As Ike prepared to
leave on a promised Korean inspection tour shortly after he
won election that November, the Washington* Daily News
*applauded his forthcoming leadership. America under Tru-
man, the paper editorialized, had chosen defeat in Korea
"when the State Department and the British Foreign office
brought about the recall of Gen. Douglas MacArthur and
forbade our Air Force the right to attack the enemy's Man-
churian bases." This prompted Truman to write* Daily News
editor John T. O'Rourke this unmailed spasm.

Nov. 28, '52

Dear John:

The attached editorial — it contains a double barrelled bare faced lie which I've marked with a red line.

I fired the great MacArthur for insubordination and for his effort to tie us up in an all out war in Asia.

I took a 14,000 [*mile*] air trip in order to have an understanding with him. He told me that the Korean situation was under control, that the Chinese would not come in, that he would release one of our regular divisions for occupation duty in Germany on Jan. 1 and that he would not further make a "chump" — his word not mine, out of himself by dabbling in Republican politics.

I believed him. I'd no more than arrived home when Joe Martin published Mac's letter to him.

I called in Acheson for State, Marshall for defense, and two other gentlemen. I asked their opinions on the latest piece of insubordination of God's right hand man.

They gave them. I said not a word about the action I intended to take, which was, of course, to recall him and relieve him of all his commands.

State and Defense opposed immediate action; the other two gentlemen were of the opinion that Mac should be taken off his seat next to God.

We had another meeting. State (Acheson) still opposed relieving the so called "great" General. Defense (Marshall) had read all the messages over the years to and from the President and MacArthur, and had come to the conclusion that he should be relieved.

Then I told the four of them that I'd intended to fire him when we first met but that I expressed no opinion because I wanted the unbiased opinions of the men I trusted.

Britain nor anyone else ever entered the picture.

State (Acheson) still advised that the uproar would be terrific and I should consider the matter further.

I fired MacArthur for insubordination and a mis-statement of the facts to me at Wake.

Of course, truth means not one thing to Roy Howard or your snotty little News — but these are the facts.

Harry S. Truman

Truman's temper flared again a week later when the same newspaper claimed that the United States was "kow towing" to Russia in the current debate over a Korean settlement. "Fortunately," sighed the Washington Daily News, *"time is running out on Secretary of State Dean Acheson and company, and this may be the last time they can sell the United States down the river."*

The outgoing President yielded to, then abandoned, the temptation to send the Daily News *editorial to his other capital city nemesis, Eugene Meyer's Washington* Post.

Dec. 4, 1952

To: Philip L. Graham
From: The White House

Look at the attached editorial from Roy Howard's snotty little News. It should have appeared in Eugene Meyer's paper.

"How come" it didn't?

H.S.T.

A Korean armistice was signed the summer after Truman left the White House. Despite his campaign rhetoric of the year before, in which he sounded much like Douglas MacArthur on world affairs, Eisenhower accepted a status quo antebellum — *two Koreas separated at roughly the same place as before, the 38th parallel.*

Truman had intended to unify Korea; that's why he had given MacArthur the green light to march into the North. Red Chinese intervention and Truman's decision not to risk a world war had prevented unification, of course, but HST clung to his original design after leaving Washington — as seen in an unmailed letter he wrote to South Korea's former national police chief.

November 4, 1954

My dear Chief Choi:

Thank you very much for your letter of October twentieth. I am always hoping that the Republic of Korea will come out as the whole Republic of the Peninsula. I am sure that eventually that will happen. I know you are doing all you can toward that end.

Sincerely yours,

Looking back over the Truman era, New York Times *Washington correspondent Arthur Krock reflected in his memoirs, "Truman was the one President, who, though I wrote as critically about him as I have about any other, never held it against me personally." Krock was wrong; he just had not received the complaints Truman wrote him. Toward the end of his presidency, the testy Missourian nearly mailed the* Times *correspondent a sweeping defense of his foreign policy. His letter to Krock was sealed, its envelope addressed. Both letter and torn envelope were found among the President's papers.*

September 11, 1952

Personal & Confidential

Dear Arthur:

In your column this morning, you speak of gross and costly blunders of the Truman Administration in foreign policy. Wish you would be specific and name them.

Was the salvation of Greece and Turkey a blunder? Was the Berlin Air-lift a blunder? Was the economic recovery of free Europe with our assistance a blunder? Was the military rehabilitation and strengthening of the free world a blunder? Was the European Alliance (N.A.T.O.) a blunder? Was the rehabilitation of the Philippine Republic a blunder? Were the Japanese Treaty and the Pacific Agreements blunders?

Chiang Kai-shek's downfall was his own doing. His field Generals surrendered the equipment we gave him to the Commies and used his own arms and ammunition to overthrow him. Only an American Army of 2,000,000 men could have saved him, and that would have been World War III.

Now where and what are the blunders?

Foreign policy has been costly. But World World III would be ten times as costly.

The appropriations for Greece and Turkey and the Marshall Plan and also for the Military Plan were voted by bipartisan majorities in Congress, which made them approved National Policies.

The Treaties were overwhelmingly approved.

I've always thought Arthur Krock to be intellectually honest. But when you contribute to the breakup of the foreign policy of the United States, you help bring on World War III. When you do it by misleading and untrue statements — well it is almost as bad for the country as McCarthyism.

You can disagree all you want on any subject, farm, labor, monetary, debt control or foreign policy and I won't care at all — if, if you tell the truth.

> Sincerely,
> Harry S. Truman

Asia held additional trauma for America after Truman left office. On Red China's southern flank, France's old colonial empire in Indochina crumbled. From its ruins emerged a North Vietnamese regime, which Washington considered a kindred soul to the Communist dictatorship in Peking. President John F. Kennedy sent military advisers to shore up South Vietnam's defense. Seemingly wiser, Presi-

dent Lyndon B. Johnson, equating Vietnam with Korea, sent Marines, infantry, and B-52 bombers.

Truman, fond of LBJ since the Texas Democrat's senatorial days, also saw parallels between Korea and Vietnam, and in a press statement supported Johnson's escalation of U.S. involvement there. He called LBJ's critics "side-line hecklers," and accused America's reluctant allies (principally Britain and France) of having "short memories." They were, Truman said, "turning their backs on us" in Vietnam.

Even when the war, with its guerrilla style of fighting, proved far different from Truman's Korean experience, the Missourian backed Johnson's decisions. Johnson flew to Guam in 1967 for a strategy meeting, and Truman, with memories of the Wake Island meeting with General MacArthur, issued a statement urging "full support" for the President's "stand against aggression."

Then something happened. The following year, when old friend and former Truman aide Charlie Murphy sent the now-ailing former President a similar statement suggesting that he release it over his signature, word came back that Mr. Truman "did not wish to make a statement at this time." Perhaps it was politics. Hubert Humphrey, Johnson's Vice-President, was seeking the Democratic presidential nomination that summer, and Democrats were playing down the war effort to soften criticism over LBJ's hard line in Vietnam. Their efforts failed, however, and Republican Richard Nixon defeated Humphrey, even though Johnson de-escalated the war and sought a negotiated settlement.

During Nixon's first year as President, Vietnam peace negotiations in Paris bogged down, partly out of American design. Among other things, Nixon wanted to buy time to shift responsibility for the fighting in Vietnam from American to South Vietnamese forces. This strategy angered Clark Clifford, onetime Truman presidential assistant, who, as Lyndon Johnson's Defense Secretary, had helped convince

LBJ to move to the negotiating table. To prod the Nixon Administration in Paris, Clifford wrote, in an article in Foreign Affairs, *"Let us start to bring our men home — and let us start* now."

Clifford sent his old boss a copy of the article, asking Truman to comment. Although certainly no admirer of Nixon, Truman didn't approve of Clifford's tactic. It probably reminded him of MacArthur. Clifford, however, never learned about it. Written three and a half years before his death, HST's reply is the last piece of unmailed correspondence to surface in his personal papers.

[Late June 1969]

Dear Clark:

I was glad to have your letter of June 18th, and the reprint of your article in Foreign Affairs Quarterly.

Since you asked me to comment, I will do so, briefly.

The question that comes to mind is whether this article at this time will help to expedite the Paris and private negotiations, and hasten the cease fire and the peace. Another question is whether it might not have been more useful to give the benefit of your views and judgment to the Administration first.

With all good wishes.

Sincerely yours,

Chapter 5

RUNNING THE GOVERNMENT

Diary Entries, 1949

Thursday, March 24

Mr. Churchill is coming to dinner. . . . This Blair-Lee House is a handicap to such events. . . . How we need the old building across the street, known as the White House. If Theodore Roosevelt and old man Coolidge had done as they should, we wouldn't be out doors now! Mr. Kim Meade White[1] did a botch job in 1902 and [*Coolidge*] the silent ? old man from Mass. did a worse one in 1927. It's hell. None of the Roosevelt tribe gave a damn about the official residence. They were all promoters for themselves, I'm sorry to say.

Sunday, March 27

Margie came home (not home, she came down to D.C.) on Wednesday so she could attend Winnie's dinner.[2] Margie

---

[1] Charles F. McKim of the architectural firm McKim, Mead and White oversaw reconstruction of the White House's main floor in 1902.

[2] "Margie" was the President's nickname for his daughter, Margaret. "Winnie" is Winston Churchill.

had a cold and couldn't work in N.Y., that is really why she came. We, Margie and I, went for a walk at about 2 P.M. Had a grand time watching the reaction of the people. They were never sure that they were seeing what they really saw. All were smilingly polite but one damned sailor. He sat with his feet out in the way while we passed but his girl stood up, smiled and saluted.

Friday, September 2

Usual appointments after a Cabinet meeting with no controversy. It took up only fifteen minutes! Usually takes an hour. Saw a Louisiana Judge, Guston L. Porperi, who'd been holding court in N.Y. A fine man and a friend of former Senator Overton.[3] Dick Duncan from Kansas City came in. Had a nice visit with him. I was instrumental in making him a Federal Judge. . . . Talked to Gordon Clapp, T.V.A. Administrator about a survey he will make in the Near East for the Arabs and Jews. Everyone I've sent to this territory comes back hoping he'll never have any more contact with Jews! I told Clapp to make an economic survey in the interest of the world peace situation.

Saturday, October 22

81st Congress quits after one hell of a session. The disappointed Republicans tried every strategy to ruin the session. Even the "good" ones joined the Dixiecrats of the Byrd, Ellender, McClellan stripe to defeat *a* program. They failed.

Tuesday, November 1

I have another hell of a day. Look at my appointment list! It is only a sample of the whole year. Trying to make the 81st Congress perform is and has been worse than cussing the 80th. A President never loses prestige fighting Congress.

---

[3] John H. Overton, U.S. Senator from Louisiana.

And I can't fight my own Congress. There are some terrible chairmen in the 81st. But so far things have come out *fairly* well. I've kissed more consarned S.O.B. so-called Democrats and left wing Republicans than all the Presidents put together. I have very few people fighting my battles in Congress as I fought F.D.R.'s.

Running the government was frustrating business for Harry Truman. The American system of checks and balances grated against his decisive and compulsive nature. When his own political party controlled Capitol Hill, long-tenured rural and southern Democrats defied him like feudal barons. When Republicans outnumbered Democrats in Congress, Truman got even less cooperation. But at least he could call them names.

During his 1948 election campaign he turned Republican legislative control into an advantage and pitched most of his speeches at the record of what he called "that do-nothing, good-for-nothing Republican 80th Congress." Someone yelled from the crowd one day, "Give 'em hell, Harry!" and that tag line endured despite the fact that in public Truman rarely used four-letter words. For one thing, no matter how aggravated he might become over congressional opposition or bureaucratic red tape, he would never curse within earshot of a woman if he could help it.

But Reverend Raymond B. Kimbrell, pastor of a Kansas City Methodist church, didn't like what he did hear from the mouth of the President, and after the 1948 campaign he wrote Truman about it. "Dear Harry," began Kimbrell's letter, which scolded him for "cussing in public," for his rigid political loyalties, his attacks on Congress, and, for good measure, the way Truman was directing the government's economic policy. We could no longer count on a 1849–style gold rush to save us from economic collapse, Kimbrell warned Truman.

The pastor, who received a brief, cordial reply from Rose Conway, never knew that his letter to "Harry" had triggered a spasm.

April 12, 1949

My dear Mr. *Kimbrell:*

Your typewritten note to me opening with "Dear Harry," is most interesting. I do not know you well enough to say "Dear Ray" to you.

The President of the United States appreciates your interest in his welfare. I am delighted as an individual to call your attention to Daniel Chapter 3 verses 47 to 49 inclusive, Esther Chapters 5 and 6 and to Matthew Chapter 26 verses 47 to 49 inclusive. All these references have to do with loyalty both to God and to people. I am somewhat surprised that a good Methodist preacher — if you are a good one — would advise the Chief Executive of this great Republic to become a double crosser. For your information, I have been and am being a successful President. The people think that too, as conclusively proved Nov. 2 '48.

The only Congress I ever damned was one that needed more than that. It was the 80th, probably with one exception, the worst in our history.

If gold in 1849 had any effect on the panic of 1873 I fail to see the connection.

Public use of emphatic language, in certain cases, is a prerogative the President will never forego. Your judgment of what makes a bigger and better man is about on a par with Horace Greeley's, old Medill McCormick's, Hearst's and James Gordon Bennett's. You should look them up. The Kansas City Star, Pearson, Life, Time, Winchell and maybe Fulton Lewis are your authorities, I presume.

Best of luck to you and may you eventually become a tolerant, honest, good religious leader.

Sincerely,

A President wears many hats; he not only functions as the head of his political party and as chief legislator, but among other things as commander-in-chief of the armed forces. In that latter capacity, Truman received an appeal from Eleanor Roosevelt for help in her humanitarian effort to assist conscientious objectors who had refused on religious grounds to enter combat during World War II. Military authorities had considered many of them imposters and had imprisoned them for dereliction of duty. Mrs. Roosevelt asked her husband's successor to forgive and forget, to grant them all a presidential pardon.

Truman struggled through three drafts of an unmailed response. His first one expressed his unvarnished feelings on the matter.

May 17, 1948

Dear Mrs. Roosevelt:

I read your letter of [*the*] thirteenth with a great deal of interest. I have thoroughly looked into the conscientious objectors case and, I think, all the honest conscientious objectors have been released.

I'll admit that it is rather difficult for me to look on a conscientious objector with patience while your four sons and my three nephews were risking their lives to save our Government, and the things for which we stand, these people were virtually shooting them in the back.

I ran across one conscientious objector that I really believe is all man — he was a young Naval Pharmacist Mate who served on Okinawa carrying wounded sailors and marines from the battle field. I decorated him with a Congressional Medal of Honor. I asked him how it came about that he as a conscientious objector was willing to go into the things of the battlefield and he said to me that he could serve the Lord and save lives as well there as anywhere else in the world.

He didn't weigh over one hundred and forty pounds and he was about five feet six inches tall. I shall never forget him.

My experience in the first world war with conscientious objectors was not a happy one — the majority of those with whom I came in contact were just plain cowards and shirkers — that is the reason I asked Justice Roberts[4] to make a complete survey of the situation and to release all those that he felt were honestly conscientious objectors and that has been done. My sympathies with the rest of them are not very strong, as you can see. I do appreciate your interest in them and can see now that all danger is passed why they would want to get out of jail.

Sincerely yours,

Congress provides the money to run the government, the President spends it. Consequently, congressmen devote a lot of energy to cross-examining people who dispense those funds, namely executive department heads. This often irked Truman. He resented the time it required for his people to be away from their desks. Then, too, he expected friendly treatment for his administrators from congressional committees chaired by fellow Democrats, but he did not always get it.

A few months after V-J Day, amid accusations that surplus U.S. war equipment worth billions of dollars had been either stolen or destroyed, Congress launched a probe. The same Senate committee on defense expenditures that one-time Senator Harry Truman had chaired, demanded that surplus-property director General Edmund B. Gregory explain the losses. Gregory's grilling before the committee elicited a Truman protest intended for committee chairman, Senator James M. Mead.

---

4   Owen J. Roberts, former associate justice on the U.S. Supreme Court.

[June 1946]

Dear Jim:

The Surplus Property Program is just about wrecked. As you remember, the Congress passed a Surplus Property Act, which was impossible of administration. It set up a Board of three men and the program was delayed six months waiting for an amendment to that Act so that an Administrator could take it over and operate it.

It was impossible to get any person to accept the responsibility of Surplus Property Program because everyone knew it would be a headache, with all the impossible priorities which are contained in the measure and with the surplus property scattered from one end of the world to the other.

I finally drafted General Gregory who was Quartermaster General during the war and who did one of the outstanding jobs, as you know, in the whole war setup. The General didn't want the job. The reason for this letter is a few days ago before your Committee a bunch of "kikes" from New York and Senator Wherry from Nebraska and Councillor Meador treated General Gregory in a most discourteous manner. It was entirely uncalled for — the General has decided to walk out as Surplus Administrator and I don't blame him.

Now I am suggesting that you, Meador or Wherry come up here and run the Surplus Property Program. If you are going to browbeat the only decent help I can get and give them no protection when they appear before your committee, there just isn't a chance to get that thing to operate.

I regret the necessity for this letter very much but unless the Committees of the Congress are willing to give me a little better cooperation than they have since the war ceased with Japan, it is an impossibility to meet the administrative situations which have been created by the Congress itself.

Truman also bristled when questioned about the wisdom of his appointments to various government jobs. Merlo Pusey of the Washington Post wanted him to expand upon a Time article about how and why he named Fred M. Vinson Chief Justice of the United States, in 1946. Truman's explanation was, however, assigned to his secretary's file cabinet.

May 6, 1950

Dear Mr. Pusey:

Charlie Ross handed me your letter of the first. The facts in the case are —

After Chief Justice Stone died, of course, it was necessary for me to appoint a Chief Justice to take his place. I myself made a survey of all the Federal Circuit Judges and a number of State Court Judges endeavoring to find the proper man to fill his place at that time. A short time after Justice Stone's death, or just before he died, a controversy was going on between Mr. Justice Jackson and Mr. Justice Black. Jackson at that time was in Germany acting as United States Chief Counsel at the war criminal trials. I decided that I would talk with Justice Hughes with whom he was well acquainted. I phoned him I would like to come out to see him and he said he would immediately come down to see me, which he did within the hour. We discussed a great number of Federal Circuit Judges and all the justices on the Supreme Court at that time with a view to deciding on a Chief Justice. Mr. Hughes finally wound up his conversation by saying that in his opinion the best man for the place would be my Secretary of the Treasury, who at that time was Fred M. Vinson. These are the facts and just as the conversation took place.

I had a similar conversation with Mr. Justice Roberts. I telephoned him at Philadelphia asking him to drop by and see me the first time he happened to be in Washington. After making the same sort of survey as Mr. Chief Justice Hughes and I had made, he made exactly the same recommendation that Chief Justice Hughes had made.

The article in Time with regard to Chief Justice Hughes is exactly as set out in your communication. He was very much embarrassed by the article appearing in that character assassination sheet and I understood perfectly what had happened. There never was an abler man or a more ethical one than Chief Justice Hughes.

Sincerely yours,

When Clinton P. Anderson of New Mexico, whom Truman had appointed Secretary of Agriculture, resigned in 1948 to run for the United States Senate, Truman felt sorely abused. He believed Anderson had abandoned his cabinet post that year because he figured that Thomas E. Dewey was a shoo-in to win the presidency. After Truman's political ship stayed miraculously afloat in that election, the newly seated Senator Anderson wrote his former mentor about his troubles. Truman almost sent Anderson a letter in kind.

September 24, 1949

Dear Clint:

Thanks for your letter of the twenty-second. I hope the situation will straighten out.

I've been receiving rumors and information about the situation in the Senate with regard to the Executive Pay Bill. Much to my surprise they tell me that you are against it and made the statement that most of the people are overpaid anyway. I really didn't expect that from you, if that is true.

There is nothing in the world that I need more than able men and in order to get those able men they must have enough money to pay their living expenses in the city of Washington. Most of them are men who can do from two to five times as well, as far as salaries are concerned, in private industry. You know the vast majority of them and you know they are honest, conscientious and hard working people. I thought your sympathy was with them.

Sincerely yours,

Harry

A commission led by former President Herbert Hoover to study government operations issued its report in early 1950 with recommendations for bureaucratic reorganization. "I am taking that report for what it means . . ." Truman said after he sent Congress twenty-one reorganization plans to enhance government efficiency. Both the Senate and the House had to approve them, and in the Senate, John L. Mc-Clellan (D.-Ark.), who chaired a key committee, questioned the President's motives. At a White House press conference, a reporter asked: "Mr. President, will you comment on Senator McClellan's charge that you are using those reorganization proposals as an excuse for a power grab —" Truman interrupted, "The only comment I can make is that it just isn't true."

The President strode out of the conference and asked Miss Conway to take dictation. Before he could dispatch his letter to John McClellan, however, the Senator, with a change of heart, telephoned HST with assurances of his support.

May 22, 1950

Dear John:

I am somewhat at a loss to understand just what the Senate means when it talks economy and then proceeds to cripple every measure for the economic operation of the Government that is sent to the Congress by the Executive Department. It seems that you are the leader in an attempt to sabotage nearly every reorganization plan that is sent to the Senate and I am sincerely sorry that that is the case.

The Commission on the reorganization of the Executive Branch of the Government was set up after I had signed a bill authorizing it. It was a bipartisan commission headed by Herbert Hoover for the Republicans and Dean Acheson for the Democrats. They spent an immense amount of money and an untold amount of labor in presenting a report which I have been trying religiously to implement. All the satisfaction I've been able to get out of the more than seventy per cent accomplishment is to be charged with trying to grab power, which has no foundation and fact. I understand that you made that statement.

Now I shall proceed to recommend reorganization plans to carry out the complete report of the Commission which went into the organization of the Executive Branch of the Government and I shall continue to send them to the Congress as long as I am President of the United States. If you want to take the responsibility yourself of crippling the operation of the Government of the United States you will have to assume that responsibility now and historically also.

I regret that you are not yourself familiar with the operations of the Government of the United States. If you had had a little administrative experience I think you would understand what a handicap it is when every effort for efficiency and economy is stymied not only because of a poor organizational setup but because of a lack of cooperation of the people who ought to be wholeheartedly for such a procedure.

I hope you will give a little more careful consideration to future reorganization plans which I send to the Congress and that we may finally wind up with some approach to efficiency and economy in the running of the Government.

Sincerely yours,

Relations between Truman and Democratic committee chairmen turned worse during his last year in office. "I do not care to comment on congressional committees. It might

*not be printable," he snapped. Over the next several months
the President wrote two complaints he never mailed, one to
Franklin D. Roosevelt, Jr., then serving on the House For-
eign Affairs Committee, and the other to former U.S. Senator
Burton K. Wheeler, with whom Truman had served in the
Senate.*

[February 15, 1952]

Dear Franklin:

I appreciated most highly your letter of the seventh regarding the Economy Act of 1952 and the action which you are
proposing to take with several other Senators [*sic*]. I hope
you will follow this to a successful conclusion.

One of the difficulties at this end of the street is the fact
that the Secretary of Defense, Secretary of the Treasury and
the Secretary of State are almost constantly before Committees when the Congress is in session.

Secretary Lovett has appeared before four or five Committees since the Congress met and made almost identical
statements. He was asked almost identical questions by each
Committee. I can't see why in the world one hearing before
one Committee wouldn't be enough and that would give the
Secretary of Defense a chance to carry out his job.

That same procedure has been followed with the Secretary
of the Army, Secretary of the Navy and the Secretary of the
Air Force.

Dean Acheson has spent the whole time since Congress
has been in session appearing before Committees. You would
think the Foreign Relations of the Senate and Foreign Affairs
Committee of the House would be the Committees to obtain
this information from the Secretary of State but that does
not seem to be the case.

The Secretary of the Treasury has spent the whole time
since Congress came back before the two Banking and Cur-
rency Committees of the House and Senate, the Finance

Committee of the Senate and the Ways and Means Committee of the House, reporting over and over again the same statements and answering the same questions. This not only wastes the time of the men who have to work almost day and night to keep the Departments running but it piles up a lot of useless records which eventually are destroyed.

It seems to me that one or two first class hearings in the House and Senate with a printed record of the Committees could be passed around and save all this waste of time.

I think you are on the right track with regard to the Budget where the same procedure is followed on appropriations.

All these Cabinet members in addition to appearances before Legislative Committees will appear again and repeat the same procedure before subcommittees of the Appropriations Committees of the House and Senate and then in all probability will have to appear again before the full Committees on Appropriations of the House and Senate. It is a frustrating procedure and anything that you gentlemen in the Senate and House can do to save the time and the nerves of the Cabinet Members will be highly appreciated by me.

Sincerely yours,

April 28, 1952

Dear Burt:

I more than appreciate your letter of the twenty-fifth about railroad bonds and securities being placed without public bidding. You and I have always thought that was wrong. I still think it is. As a matter of public service I'll make a statement on the subject one of these days which I think will put the Interstate Commerce Commission back on the track.

There is another matter in which I am extremely interested and one to which I wish you would give a lot of thought. The Senate and House Committees have been following the procedure that is as contrary to the Bill of Rights as old Jeffers' Star Chamber was to the Rights of the Individual.[5]

I wonder if there is not some way we can get the actions of certain Committees into the Courts. They now have me in the Court and I don't object to it at all.[6] McCarren's Committee with himself, Ferguson and Willis Smith have been calling members of the Administration Staff before them and browbeating them unmercifully.[7]

The Finance Committee, with Walter George presiding, and Millikin and one or two others called in the Collector of Internal Revenue at Kansas City, just because he happened to be in my home town and an appointee of mine, and browbeat the poor fellow into nervous prostration.

Don't you think that a Grand Jury could support the Bill of Rights by perhaps indicting these gentlemen for tearing up the Constitution?

I wish you would look into it and come to see me some day and we will talk about it.

Sincerely yours,

Senator George's committee treated Kansas City's Collector of Internal Revenue roughly because the IRS was under scrutiny for corruption within its ranks. From outside the government, Francis Biddle, Franklin Roosevelt's Attorney General, whom Truman had dropped, and who now chaired the liberal Americans for Democratic Action (ADA), watched the controversy with more than passing interest. At

---

[5] A sham tribunal used by the throne in Tudor England to judge its enemies guilty, headed at one time by Lord Chief Justice George Jeffreys.

[6] To abort a steel strike Truman seized the steel mills. Opponents appealed his action to the U.S. Supreme Court.

[7] Pat McCarran (D.-Nev.), chairman of the Senate Judiciary Committee, along with Homer Ferguson (R.-Mich.) and Willis Smith (D.-N.C.), led the Senate inquiry into Truman's steel seizure.

*the scandal's height, he needled Truman with an ADA press
release critical of the White House's IRS reform efforts. The
President jumped to the defense, but he later decided, "Just
file the whole thing. No answer necessary."*

January 16, 1952

Dear Francis:

I read your release of January 11 with a great deal of interest and, of course, I appreciate most highly your interest
in public service and the welfare of the country. You know
from experience as Attorney General that it is a difficult position to fill efficiently. I hope we can find an answer to our
difficulties.

Ninety-nine and nine tenths per cent of the employees of
the Federal Government are decent, honest people. The one-
tenth of one per cent has been the cause of our difficulties
and wherever we've found laxity drastic action has been
taken.

People who are employed to handle money, whether in
banks, business houses or Government, are subject to immense pressures and temptation. The vast majority of them
do the job as it should be done but a constant check is necessary. There have been immense bank defalcations in the last
year from the inside. Most of the people who have gone
wrong have been caught and the shortages have been met
either by insurance or Federal Deposit Insurance Corporation. We can't talk about things like that because people
might lose confidence in their financial institutions and, as
you know, there has been no loss to a depositor in any bank
under the Federal Deposit Insurance Corporation in the last
ten years — a record which is without parallel.

As you know, I do not countenance malfeasance in office
and before we are through I think we will be entirely satisfied
with the result. I have had some sorry disappointments with

people who have promised to help on things of that kind and then have publicly gone back on me when it came time to operate.

I hope that everything is going well with you and that 1952 will be a great year for you.

Sincerely yours,

Truman demonstrated on another occasion that disgruntled former cabinet members and probing congressional committees were not alone in sitting in judgment of the White House. HST himself held strong negative feelings toward many cabinet members whom he had inherited from Roosevelt. When, with Truman's blessing, Jonathan Daniels began work on a biography of him, Truman jotted Daniels "some facts" about the Roosevelt crowd. Because Truman no doubt realized later that Daniels had also worked for Roosevelt, having served as FDR's press secretary, he decided finally to withhold his observations.

February 26, 1950

Dear Jonathan:

I wonder if you have thought to go into the background and ability of each member of the cabinet and those who sat with the cabinet which I inherited on April 12, 1945. It should make an interesting chapter in your book. Maybe I shouldn't bring the subject to your attention, but as I look back on that situation it makes me shudder. I am sure that God Almighty had me by the hand. He must have had a personal interest in the welfare of this great Republic.

There was Stettinius, Sec. of State — a fine man, good looking, amiable, cooperative, but never an idea new or old; Morgenthau, block head, nut — I wonder why F.D.R. kept him around. Maybe you know. He fired himself from my cabinet by threatening what he'd do to me under certain circumstances. Then there was Stimson, a real man — honest, straightforward and a statesman sure enough. Francis Biddle, attorney general — you make your own analysis. Frank Walker, P.M.G. — my kind of man, honest, decent, loyal — but no new ideas. Miss Perkins, Sec. of Labor, a grand lady — but no politician. F.D.R. had removed every bureau and power she had. Then Henry Wallace, Sec. of Commerce, who had no reason to love me or to be loyal to me. Of course he wasn't loyal. "Honest" Harold Ickes who was never for anyone but Harold, would have cut F.D.R.'s throat — or mine for his "high minded" ideas of a headline — and did. Agriculture's Wickard, a nice man, who never learned how his department was set up. Then there was Leo Crowley, whose sense of honor was minus and Chester Bowles, price control man, whose idea of administration was conversation with crazy columnists. Thank God Fred Vinson was there as O.W.M.R. and Bill Davis as Chairman of the Labor Board.

But, Jonathan, there was not a man in the list who would talk frankly at a Cabinet meeting! The honest ones were afraid to and the others wanted to fool me anyhow.

Am I wrong? Take a look and see how and in what manner they left me. Poor Forrestal, you'll have to evaluate yourself. He never could make a decision. Harold Smith, A-1 conniver.

"Poor Forrestal," former defense secretary James V. Forrestal, committed suicide in May 1949. To commemorate him, Massachusetts businessman Bradley Dewey sent Truman a suggestion for a suitable memorial. The President thought Dewey's idea silly and turned his serious suggestion into a humorous counterproposal. By not mailing it, Truman probably avoided serious repercussions.

June 13, 1949

Dear Brother Dewey:

Change the name of the Pentagon to the "Forrestal Building"? — not a bad idea. While we are about it, let's get rid of a lot of other mossback names; we could call Faneuil Hall in Boston the Curley Building. Independence Hall in Philadelphia might appropriately bear the distinguished name of Joe Guffey.

Looking around Washington, it seems to me that we should change the name of the Social Security Building to the Townsend Building, in recognition of an eminent contemporary reformer.

Nor should we ignore history. The Temple of the Department of Justice might properly be called the Boss Tweed Building as a friendly gesture towards New York. I will speak to John Snyder with a view to naming his headquarters [*the Treasury Building*] the Charles Ponsi Building, or better still — name it for the originator of the Pyramid Clubs. And for good measure let's call the Library of Congress the Joe Louis Athenaeum. I really think you and Bill Jeffers have come up with something: a noble experiment — to coin a phrase — with infinite possibilities.

Very sincerely yours,

Concerning government buildings, the White House, long in need of renovation, was reconstructed by Truman, complete with the addition of a controversial south balcony. He made his first move to renovate the White House in 1946, when he announced plans to expand the adjoining executive office wing. Public protest followed, and the Senate procrastinated on funding the expansion.

When Senator Theodore F. Green [D.-R.I.] petitioned Truman to appoint a constituent of his to a new government post, HST, in an unmailed reply, vented anger over the Senate's recalcitrance on his office expansion plan, and for its rough handling of recent nominees of his own for presidential appointments. The Senate had just refused confirmation of oil man Edwin W. Pauley, while confirming after stormy deliberation appointments for George E. Allen and James K. Vardaman, Jr.

April 4, 1946

Dear Senator:

I appreciated very much your letter of the second in regard to Mr. L. Metcalfe Walling and I am more than happy to have a recommendation from you for this Board. I have a large number of people under consideration but I am expecting to be in no hurry making the appointment. The Senate has been so balky here of late on appointments and requests from the President that I see no reason for hurrying these matters up.

I can't understand why the Senate would prevent the President from having the necessary office space to transact his business and having it available where he could get to it. I never heard as much assinine conversation in my life about purported abasement of The White House, and the action which was taken on Pauley, Allen and Vardaman rather makes me feel as if a great many Senators are more interested in hampering the program of the President, than in helping him. As far as I am concerned, I can still take it and will go along and do the best I can under the circumstances.

I'll be glad to give Mr. Walling every consideration possible but, as I said before, I am not making this appointment hurriedly and it will be some time before the man for this place is named. I do, however, appreciate your interest.

Sincerely yours,
Harry S. Truman

Truman also ran into a snag when he tried to obtain Senate confirmation of Mon Wallgren, his friend since Senate

days, to head up a national mobilization board. The appoint-
ment stalled when Wallgren's bitter home-state opponent,
Republican Senator Harry P. Cain, claimed that while Wall-
gren served as Governor of Washington State he had been
influenced by Communists. Although Democrat Millard
Tydings, whose committee was to rule on the confirmation,
assured Truman that he was doing everything possible to
help, the President's patience wore thin, so thin that he nearly
mailed this complaint.

March 4, 1949

My dear Millard:

I received your message last night about our friend Mon
Wallgren. I wonder if you remember a certain controversy
over a mutual friend and an efficient public servant by the
name of Perlman?[8]

You, as a Senator know all there is to know about Mon.
You know that he is honest; you know that he is an able
executive; you know that he is capable of filling the position
to which I have appointed him.

There will be no retreat on my part and I had expected
none on yours. Were our positions reversed, Mon's confirmation would go through. I know that you can put it
through and I am requesting you, as a personal favor to put
it through.

The Senate will have come to a pretty pass when it lets a
minority political scalawag run the majority.

As far as I am concerned the fight goes to the bitter end.

Sincerely,

Harry S. Truman

P.S. Millard: This letter is neither personal nor confidential — it's for the record if it will help you.

HST

---

8 Philip B. Perlman, Solicitor General, whose confirmation was delayed
in 1949 by opposition from Republican Senator Homer Ferguson.

The bitter end of this controversy came nearly three months later when Truman withdrew his friend's name, after charge and countercharge. Representative Adolph Sabath quickly submitted his own roster of candidates for the vacant position. The President filed away his intended response.

May 25, 1949

Dear Adolph:

Thanks for yours of the twenty-third recommending men to fill the position to which I wished to place Mon Wallgren.

I don't see much use of making that appointment any time soon — the Congress seems to be in a bad frame of mind. When our own Rules Committee ties up legislation, just as it did in the 80th Congress, what can a President expect.

Sincerely yours,

Harry S. Truman

To stop a steel strike in 1952, Truman seized the steel mills. All hell broke loose and the U.S. Supreme Court declared Truman's action unconstitutional. Perhaps to smooth over strained relations between the judiciary and executive branches of government, liberal Supreme Court Justice William O. Douglas wrote Truman a letter. He was leaving the capital temporarily, Douglas explained, and he regretted not being able to discuss election-year Democratic politics with Truman beforehand. Douglas did not, however, mention the court's recent anti-Truman steel ruling. Truman did, in his never-mailed reply.

July 9, 1952

Dear Bill:

I appreciated very much your letter of July third,[9] and I am sorry that I didn't have a chance to talk with you before

---

9 Douglas' letter, stapled to Truman's unmailed reply, was actually dated July 1.

you left. In fact, I am sorry that I didn't have an opportunity to discuss precedents with you before you came to the conclusion you did on that crazy decision that has tied up the country.

I am writing a monograph on just what makes Justices of the Supreme Court tick. There was no decision by the majority although there were seven opinions against what was best for the country.

I don't see how a Court made up of so-called "Liberals" could do what that Court did to me. I am going to find out just why before I quit this office.

Sincerely yours,
Harry S. Truman

Judging from the number of undispatched letters and memos he filed away during his last year as President, Truman in 1952 felt more testy than usual. The letter to Douglas was only one of over two dozen he wrote that year, and on subjects that range over the entire scope of this volume. Another among them reveals Truman's disgust with what he considered bureaucratic ineptitude.

September 17, 1952

Memorandum for: Mrs. Ruth B. Shipley
                Passport Division
                State Department
From: The President
In April 1952 Hon. Max Lowenthal requested a visa to visit Italy and Sicily. On September 3rd he was refused a visa.

Mr. Lowenthal was counsel to the Interstate Commerce Committee when the Railway Finance investigation was carried on by Senator Wheeler and myself. He was also the counselor when the same Committee held the famous Hold-

ing Company hearings. Both these hearings resulted in fundamental legislation:

> The Transportation Act of 1940; known as the Wheeler-
> Truman Bill and the Holding Company Act which
> broke up such crooked organizations as Insull's and
> Hopson's.

Mr. Lowenthal furnished the legal knowledge necessary for
the hearings and the bills.

While Mr. Lowenthal's application was pending you
promptly issued visas to Westbrook Pegler and to Kolberg.[10]
Pegler is a louse. All he wanted to do was to write a tissue
of lies about the foreign policy for Hearst and the sabotage
press. Yet he received prompt service from you.

Kolberg is next door to a number one traitor. He is the mov-
ing spirit in the China Lobby, and has spent the last four
years trying to discredit the State Department. He received
prompt service from you.

I want a report in writing and I want it *promptly* as to why
an honorable decent citizen is refused a passport and a couple
of crumbs can receive passports.

After Truman left public office and returned to Inde-
pendence, he still kept tabs on government operations. And,
as before, he became agitated when bureaucrats insisted
upon making the simple complex. Accustomed to plain
speaking and cutting through to the core of a matter, he got
fed up when in 1961 he came across a U.S. Treasury report
he had to decipher. This is his unmailed complaint.

---

[10]   Alfred Kohlberg, Treasurer of the American China Policy Association.

December 26, 1961

To the Treasurer of the United States

Dear Sir:

I have been reading the statement of Dec. 13, 1961, the last one I have received.

I'd appreciate it if you could find a way to place debits and credits so an ordinary citizen like myself could understand what you are trying to show.

When I am through looking and figuring what you mean I have to set up my own statement.

Why don't you set up yours so any citizen who understands debit from credit can know what you are doing. I don't think that the financial advisor of God Himself would be able to understand what the financial position of the Government of the United States is, by reading your statement.

And I have been going through them and trying to find out what they mean for twenty seven years! I found out but it took all day and half the night to do it. Make your statement a simple bookkeeping document so that any of us can understand it!

H.S.T.

Chapter 6

HUMAN GREED
AND
HUMAN NEED

Diary Entries
[Ca. 1930]

Went into business all enthusiastic. Lost all I had and all I could borrow. Mike Pendergast[1] picked me up and put me into politics and I've been lucky. I'm still an idealist and I still believe that Jehovah will reward the righteous and punish the wrongdoers. . . . Have tried to make Jackson County's Government ideal as far as the practical operation will allow. . . . Oh! If I were only John D. [*Rockefeller*] or Mellon or Wait Phillips. I'd make this section (six counties) the world's real paradise. What's the use wishing. I'm still going to do it. . . .

[Ca. 1931]

I have always believed in Santa Claus I guess. It was my opinion until my association with Barr, Vrooman and Bash[2] that most men had a sense of honor. Now I don't know.

---

[1] Father of James Pendergast, Truman's World War I buddy.
[2] Truman's fellow Jackson County judges, Robert W. Barr, Howard J. Vrooman, and Thomas B. Bash.

"The Boss"[3] says that instead of most men being honest most of them are not when they are put into a position where they can get away with crookedness. I guess I've been wrong in my premise that 92% are ethically honest. Maybe 92% are not thieves but it is a certainty that 92% are not ethically honest. . . .

We've spent $7,000,000 in [*Jackson County*] bonds and $700,000 in [*Kansas City*] revenue in my administration. I could have had [*for myself*] $1,500,000. I haven't $150. Am I a fool or an ethical giant? I don't know. The Boss in his wrath at me because his crooked contractors got no contracts said I was working to give my consulting engineer a nationwide reputation and that my honor wouldn't be a pinch of snuff. I don't care if I get honor, if the taxpayer's money goes on the ground [*for roads*] or into the buildings it's intended for. I hope that there are no more bond issues and no more trouble until I'm done and then maybe I can run a filling station or something until I've run my three score & ten and go to a quiet grave. . . .

March 26, 1949

. . . Margie and I go to the movie room at the White House and I make a broadcast for the Federal Council of Churches of Christ in America. Hope it did some good. . . .

September 2, 1949

. . . Basil O'Connor[4] came in and gave me a song and dance on infantile paralysis. It's a terrible disease but he wanted me to make a money broadcast for him!

---

3 Thomas J. Pendergast, Mike Pendergast's brother, who headed Kansas City's Democratic political machine.
4 Franklin Roosevelt's former law partner and president of the foundation combating infantile paralysis.

Arkansas Speech
July 2, 1952

The special interests that have fought against flood control and power development are teamed up with the special interests that have fought against price supports for farm products. These same special interest lobbies have fought against minimum wages for the working people. They have fought against advances in housing and health and education.

They keep yapping about "socialism" and a lot of other silly slogans to try and stop every measure for the good of the people.

Well, we have been fighting them, and we have been licking them, that kind of opposition — for 20 years we have been doing that. And I don't think we're going to stop now. . . .

County government or federal, no matter: Harry Truman learned that some people have to be restrained, others helped. Given a free hand, the powerful and greedy leave little for the needy. While he championed those American beliefs in competitive free enterprise, Truman nevertheless considered himself the little guy's elected benefactor. Call him a humanist, liberal, or progressive, Truman's social philosophy boiled down to this: the high hats with their money and their power have their lobbies working in government to get them more. The common citizen had only him.

Truman went to Washington in 1935. President Franklin Roosevelt's depression-fighting New Deal had reached high tide, and as a Senator, Truman voted for Roosevelt-requested consumer protection, legislation benefiting organized labor, Social Security, and funding for various unemployment projects. As President, Truman advocated more economic security. Japan surrendered on August 14, 1945. Three weeks later he sent Congress a mind-reeling postwar domestic re-

form package. "It's just a plain case of out-dealing the New Deal!" howled an angry Republican opponent. HST's most shocking proposal was to add government health insurance covering all citizens to Social Security. Other reform proposals included federal aid to public education, a government-backed housing program, and machinery to guarantee full employment. First priority after the war was given to the employment situation. Wartime federal defense spending had taken the nation out of the Great Depression, and Truman feared that reconversion to a peacetime economy might bring a return to hard times. While not giving him all he wanted, enough people on Capitol Hill shared Truman's concern over jobs to legislate a national employment bill.

But forecasts of a postwar depression proved wrong. People's wartime savings accounts bulged, and eager customers queued up to buy long-dreamed-of nylons and sugar, washing machines, and automobiles. Concerned over runaway inflation, Truman struggled to keep alive unpopular wartime economic controls and the government agency that had enforced them, the Office of Price Administration. OPA had unfrozen wages at the war's end, but Truman insisted that price controls remain. Otherwise, he warned in his January 1946 State of the Union Message, "feverish and opportunistic" business practices spawned by the hectic consumer demand for scarce goods would end in inflationary disaster. Be patient, he urged. We Americans enjoyed great abundance and economic know-how. "Business," Truman promised, "can in the future pay higher wages and sell for lower prices than ever before."

C. Donald Dallas, president of Revere Copper and Brass, Inc., took issue with the President's statement. He questioned its logic in a letter to Truman, pointing out that his industry's prices had remained frozen since 1940, when they were fixed by the OPA, while workers were free and encouraged by such a statement to demand and obtain inflationary wage increases. Truman's reaction to Dallas' complaint never got beyond his secretary's dictation notes.

[Late January 1946]

My dear Mr. Dallas:

I read your letter of January twenty-second with a great deal of interest and, of course, it is easy enough to take one phrase from a message, without considering the context or the message as a whole, and use it as a "straw man" to be the cause of all our troubles. I think if you will read the whole message, in which you found this statement, you will get a better viewpoint of what I have in mind.

Since 1820 the general price level has remained practically steady, the actual wages paid working men in industry have increased four times — that is their earnings are four times as great as they were in 1820, and that increase has been brought about by the increased production per man-hour due to technology.

I am just as sure as I can be that as [a] result of the inventions, which we succeeded in bringing forth during the war period, and on the return of the fighting men who naturally will be much more efficient physically and mentally than the children and the old people who have had to fill their places while they were gone, we will again see an increased output per man-hour.

I am very certain that if the price spiral is released, 1929 will be a mere shadow in comparison to what will happen to us. I know that most big business men, and most people who think they can profit from a price spiral, are anxious to see the lid come off. I am also very anxious to see all war controls released, as soon as possible, but I want to see the price line held until production can meet that price line and, in order to have an increased output and a greater market, mass production at higher wages and lower prices is the only answer.

It was a losing battle. Congress was in an anti-labor, pro-business mood. Truman asked it to extend OPA's life. Instead, powerful conservatives such as Southern Democrat Kenneth McKellar, president pro tempore of the Senate and chairman of the appropriations committee, jockeyed to render OPA impotent. By mid-1946 they had succeeded. Had Truman sent Senator McKellar this letter (it shows he had more faith in public-opinion polls before 1948 than after), the outcome would have probably been no different.

March 2, 1946

Dear Senator McKellar:

In our conversation yesterday about O.P.A. and the necessity for its continuance you were emphatic in stating that all your correspondence was against maintaining the O.P.A. Mine is exactly the other way and the poll which comes out Sunday made by Mr. Gallup verifies the correspondence that comes to the White House.

The difficulty, of course, is the enforcement. Naturally they have made some mistakes but that is to be expected in a job as big as the one that has had to be carried through on price control. I am just as certain as I can be that, unless we can maintain the control of food costs, clothing costs, and the costs of actual necessities which go into the home, until production is in full swing, we will have no future to look forward to except an inflationary spiral and a bursted bubble at the end of it, just as happened in the Florida land boom, just as happened after 1927, and which had a worse effect in 1932 after the 1929 blow up.

To date we have maintained a steady price for the actual cost of living but the savings and money pressure now is so great, and there are people who sincerely believe they ought to have the right to profit by a disastrous boom, that it is going to be more difficult from now on to hold that line.

Unless the Congress is in the frame of mind to cooperate wholeheartedly on this front, there isn't a chance of our getting the job done.

O.P.A. ought not to be repealed with lack of appropriations. If it is to be repealed it ought to be repealed in an orderly manner.

If you will examine this Gallup poll carefully you will see that the vast majority of the common everyday people, those who have no lobbyists employed, are the people who want price control, because they know what will happen to them if it is taken off.

Sincerely yours,

King Cotton, not hampered by rigid price controls, grew fat with speculative profits after the war. Cotton investors made quick riches as prices soared. That is, until October 1946. Within weeks, cotton fell from 38¢ to 28¢ a pound and the speculative market lost nearly a billion dollars. National Farmers Union president, James G. Patton, a liberal Truman supporter, wrote asking the President to investigate the cotton exchanges. Truman's unmailed reply follows.

December 7, 1946

Dear Jim:

I appreciated your note of December second very much and, for your information, we have been making some investigation of the cotton fluctuations.

I don't know whether you remember it or not but way back in the spring of 1946 and in the fall of 1945, I endeavored to get the cotton fellows to place cotton under the same controls as other commodities were placed for the reconversion period. They refused categorically to consider even a ceiling of thirty cents and, at that time, cotton was selling around twenty cents.

The usual thing happened and I am not so sure the very fellows I was talking to were not in the speculative market themselves and, to be frank with you, I can't shed any tears over what happened to them. Cotton now is selling above thirty cents which is, in my opinion, an excellent price.

I think when we get through with our investigation we will find nothing new but only a sort of manipulation of the market as has been customary in times past. The cotton people have been a special privileged class ever since I have been in Washington.

Sincerely yours,

Over the next two years the Republican 80th Congress accelerated economic decontrol. Truman resisted but lost. He was able, however, to hang on to an excise tax imposed on luxury items during the war. Stanley Marcus, whose Neiman-Marcus store in Dallas catered to rich tastes, complained to Truman. "Hold. Do not mail out letter," Rose Conway instructed in a note attached to the President's response.

July 12, 1949

My dear Mr. Marcus:

I read your letter of June twenty-eighth in regard to excise taxes with a great deal of interest. As you know, most of the expenditures recommended in the Federal budget are due to the fact that we had a war and those war expenditures are still the principal burden on the tax payers, but they must be paid.

The 80th Congress made a very serious mistake in passing the rich man's tax bill over the veto. I hope you will read my veto message and you will find we are faced with the condition which I was very careful to warn the Congress we would be faced with. Means must be found to meet the war incurred expenses in the budget and to decrease the national debt and that can't be done if all the revenue producing taxes are re-pealed. Nobody likes to pay taxes — a man will cry his head off over paying $100 taxes on his income, but he will go out and throw away $500 or $1000 on a poker game and say nothing about it. I guess that is the way the human animal is made. It is my business, however, to see that the country remains solvent and that is what I intend to do to the best of my ability — but the people and the Congress must help me.

Sincerely yours,
Harry S. Truman

Government price controls came back during the Korean War. Meat producers especially protested when their prices were rolled back. They had made big profits after forcing OPA off their backs prematurely in 1946, and they fought to retain a free market during the new wartime emergency. "This is just the same old fight," Truman told reporters. "Whenever you tread on the toes of somebody, he has to scream." After looking into the controversy, the House Agriculture Committee recommended that the President lift beef price controls. Truman dictated a defiant retort and signed it for mailing. But someone on the White House staff intercepted it and a toned-down version went out instead.

June 15, 1951

Dear Congressman Cooley:

I read your letter of the eleventh with a great deal of in-terest and also the findings of your Committee. I have some knowledge of cattle, cattle feeding and the operations of the packers who control the supply of beef.

I wish you had discussed the matter with me before you made your findings — you probably would have come to several different conclusions. I am sure you didn't talk to the real cattle feeders — most of them are in Illinois, Iowa, Nebraska, Missouri and Northeast Kansas. I myself have talked with a great many of them and they don't feel badly about the roll back. The only thing they feel badly about is the fact that the Big Four Packers[5] get all the benefit and make no sacrifice whatever. Everything regarding meat is in the hands of the Big Four Packers.

I wonder if any of your people ever made a trip to Chicago, Omaha, St. Joseph, Kansas City, St. Louis and Fort Worth and examined the refrigerators of the packers. It would be an interesting piece of information if you could go there without letting them know you were coming — you would find out where all the beef is if you really want to find out. This is a blackmail job and I'm not going to be browbeaten by a bunch of fellows who do not represent the cattle raisers or the cattle feeders and who are out to skin the consumers of meat out of all the traffic will bear. The eaters of meat have some rights just as well as the big interests.

Sincerely yours,
Harry S. Truman

Franklin Roosevelt had his New Deal. Harry Truman eventually called his domestic-reform agenda the Fair Deal. First sent to Congress right after the war, its outline sharpened in 1948 as Truman vied for election against Thomas E. Dewey. Indeed, his civil-rights ideas badly split his Democratic party that year. He sent Congress a special civil-rights message in February asking for antilynching laws and guarantees against job discrimination and voter restrictions. As a result, angry Southern Democrats considered HST a wild-eyed radical and they walked out on him that year.

But the American Communist party held an opposite view. The day Truman sent Congress his civil-rights message, John Gates, editor of the communist paper Daily Worker, *wired*

---

[5]   Swift, Armour, Cudahay, and Wilson.

the President a challenge. If he were not "merely playing with the sufferings of the Negro people to garner votes in November," said Gates, he could prove it without waiting for Congress. As Commander-in-Chief he had the power to abolish segregation in the armed forces.[6] *Moreover, Gates insisted that he could also order an end to various other discriminatory practices and call for the breakup of the House Committee on Un-American Activities. Truman penned three spasms, none of them used. Here is the first one.*

February 5, 1948

My dear Mr. Gates:

I read your telegram of the second with considerable interest.

You are making suggestions that could only be carried out in a country where legislative opposition can be hanged without trial; where the ordinary opponents of the Government are sent to concentration camps and whose families are punished for their beliefs; where patriots, who serve in emergency are shot as the opposition when the emergency no longer exists; where opposition leaders are assassinated by paid assassins; where free thought and free expression mean prison and slavery.

This great free country is not confused by lies and propaganda and, therefore, your suggestions are all beside the point.

In a Soviet State you would be in a concentration camp and your propaganda sheet suppressed. For that reason I'm happy that you live in a country which respects the rights of the individual and the right of free expression.

---

[6] On July 26, 1948, Truman issued an executive order establishing a commission to bring about desegregation of the armed forces. Desegregation was accomplished during his second administration.

I wonder if you have the guts to publish your telegram and my answer. You'd no doubt be liquidated if you did it.

Yours for a World Bill of Rights,

"I have had some bitter disappointments as President,"
Truman wrote after leaving office, "but the one that has
troubled me most, in a personal way, has been the failure to
defeat organized opposition to a national compulsory health-
insurance program." The physician membership of the Amer-
ican Medical Association labeled this Fair Deal proposal
"socialized medicine," and financed the country's most ex-
pensive and most extensive lobbying effort to defeat it.[7]
Ben Turoff, retired Ford dealer from Lee's Summit, Mis-
souri, who had known Harry since his county judge days,
agreed with the AMA's opposition. He wrote Truman that,
as it was, doctors worked too hard and "woe be unto the
poor devil that has a chronic or neurotic ailment, and even
many others," should the country take up socialized medi-
cine. Truman answered Turoff, but in an abbreviated and
more diplomatic way than in this unmailed first draft.

[April 12, 1949]

My dear Ben:

Your letter of April first is most interesting. The main difficulty is that you start off with the wrong premise. Nobody is working for socialized medicine — all my Health Program calls for is an insurance plan that will enable people to pay their doctor bills and receive hospital treatment when they need it.

---

[7]   Medicare, signed into law by President Lyndon B. Johnson in a ceremony honoring Truman at the Truman Library in 1965, contained part of HST's original design. For the story of Truman's fight with the AMA, see the editor's *Harry S. Truman Versus the Medical Lobby: The Genesis of Medicare* (Columbia: University of Missouri Press, 1979).

I can't understand the rabid approach of the American Medical Association — they have distorted and misrepresented the whole program so that it will be necessary for me to go out and tell the people just exactly what we are asking for.

When I was on the County Court in Jackson County I saw many a patient refused entrance to a hospital because he didn't have the right physician. There are just as many doctors outside the American Medical Association as there are in it and you will find every hospital is run by a clique and unless a man has the right physician he can't get into the hospital unless he is somebody of prominence or a person with a lot of money. That is all wrong in my book. I am trying to fix it so the people in the middle income bracket can live as long as the very rich and the very poor.

I am glad you wrote me because I think there are a lot of people like you who need straightening out on this subject.

Sincerely yours,

Frustrated over this and other Fair Deal recommendations stalled in Congress, Truman lashed out at the lobbies. "The selfish interests have always been working against the common good since the beginning of our history," he told a 1949 Labor Day audience. Now they used scare words like "socialism" or "welfare state" to gain their ends. "The people want a better social security system, improved education, and a national health program. The selfish interests are trying to sabotage these programs because they have no concern about helping the little fellow. . . ."

In private, HST blamed uncooperative Democratic legislative leaders as well. Federal aid to education, like health insurance, bogged down in congressional committees. Fear that "Big Brother" would dictate educational practices, and that religious schools might also receive taxpayer support, prevented action on an education bill. Patience waning, Truman nearly sent a letter upon learning that John Lesinski, Democratic chairman of the House Committee on Education and Labor, planned unexpected additional meetings to discuss the bill.

[Mid-August, 1949]

Dear [*John*]:

I received a copy of one of your notices dated August 12, 1949 on your proposed discussions on Federal Aid to Education Bill.

I tried my best to make it plain to you that the reporting of a Bill to the House is a thing I am most interested in. I am sorry that you do not appreciate my extreme interest in this piece of legislation. I don't think discussions, such as the one you are contemplating will do anything but delay and prolong the discussion and I certainly didn't expect the Chairman of the Committee on Education and Labor to join in a filibuster on one of the main bulwarks of the Democratic Platform.

I sincerely hope that you will make every endeavor to get an agreement within your Committee and report a Bill to this Session of the Congress.

One of the most terrible things that can happen is to place this Bill on a religious prejudice basis and from the debate now going on both in the Congress and in your Committee that is exactly where we are headed for. I regret it very much.

Sincerely yours,

Truman never got federal aid to education. That came first in the late fifties after the Soviet Union launched Sputnik, the world's pioneer space satellite, and Americans nearly panicked over perceived Russian advances in scientific technological achievements. By the time John Kennedy became

President, pressure had mounted to expand federal support for education, but a snag developed again over whether parochial and other private schools should receive federal aid. Kennedy opposed the idea. So did Truman, as seen in this unmailed letter to college student Marilyn M. Heinrich, who had written him for an opinion on the issue.

December 5, 1962

Dear Mrs. Heinrich:

In reply to yours of the 26th, the situation is just this. The people who run parochial schools and private schools have always been against the education of the common everyday person and that is the reason the public schools were set up.

Now, when the going gets rough, they want to cut in on the public schools which they were against.

I don't think they should have any funds that the Federal Government gives to public schools because if it wasn't for the public schools a lot of us would not have an education.

Sincerely yours,

The TVA, a vast government flood control and public power enterprise erected along the Tennessee River, stands as a monument to Franklin Roosevelt's New Deal. Truman tried to create an MVA (Missouri Valley Authority), encompassing the Missouri and upper-Mississippi river basins. He had vowed in his diary twenty years before that, even though not rich like Rockefeller, he would make the Kansas City countryside "the world's real paradise." As President, Truman expanded that vision to take in eleven states. A few scattered flood control and irrigation projects had begun along the Missouri River as part of a master plan advanced by Army Corps of Engineers chief, Major General Lewis A. Pick, and W. G. Sloan of the U.S. Department of Interior. But Truman, while favoring a stepped-up Pick-Sloan plan —

*especially after a disastrous flood hit Kansas City in 1951 —
insisted on a TVA-type program with centralized federal
direction.*

*Neither the Pick-Sloan plan nor the MVA idea had much
popular support. The region's private power companies
feared government hydroelectric competition, state officials
feared advantages might accrue to neighboring states, and
farmers simply feared the federal government. M. B. Ronald,
a Mitchell, South Dakota, newspaper publisher, who headed
a group opposed to Pick-Sloan's long-range dam construction program (they favored instead better land-management
procedures to hold water where it fell), sent Truman his
organization's position statement. The President dictated,
then withheld, a rejoinder.*

August 29, 1951

Dear Mr. Ronald:

I appreciated most highly your letter of August twenty-
third with the enclosures. I notice that you emphasized the
fact that the Pick-Sloan flood control plan would run into
the billions. While we have become accustomed here lately
to speak only of billions, the flood control program envisaged
by the Pick-Sloan plan is well under a half a billion and had
we been able to construct the reservoirs necessary to hold
back flood waters and let them run off after the first flood
crest, I am sure that Manhattan, Topeka, Lawrence and
Kansas City, Kansas and the Missouri industrial district
would not have been flooded and ruined as they were in the
late big flood. In the two Kansas Cities the damage was over
a billion dollars. Two million five hundred thousand acres
of farm land was ruined — loss, five hundred million dollars.

I want to make a suggestion to you, that you go over to
Dayton, Ohio and study the flood control program which

was constructed by Dayton and the surrounding country after the terrible flood disaster to Dayton some years ago. They have five flood control basins which are used only when it is necessary to hold water back to prevent a disaster like the one that happened to Dayton and to the Kaw Valley just recently.

I fear very much that your rain water control on farm lands would not meet the situation. It is an eye dropper remedy. I am also of the opinion that it will be necessary to have an over-all authority for the Missouri and Mississippi Valley north of Saint Louis if we expect to accomplish anything. The main difficulty in arriving at a successful plan has been that eleven states have eleven different ideas on how things should be done and all have their own selfish interests which they put above the Valley interest. Until that situation can be over come I doubt very much whether we will ever accomplish the proper development of this great Valley.

I have been working on it for thirty years and have had no cooperation whatever over the last six years when there was a real opportunity to develop the Valley in all lines — flood control, land use, navigation and power. We are losing population and losing national representation to those areas that are being properly developed. If we wait longer it will be too late.

I know the Valley and every stream in it from Saint Louis to the Minnesota and Wisconsin Lakes and from Kansas City to Yellowstone Park and from the Rockies to the Illinois River.

It is the most wonderful Valley in the world and can be made the paradise it should be if the people living in it realize what they have.

> Sincerely yours,
> Harry S. Truman

*While the conservatives who dominated Capitol Hill pro-
moted and voted for government spending projects within
their home districts, large-scale Fair Deal reform requests
like the MVA went begging. When John Rankin, senior Mississippi Democratic member of the House, wired the President asking his backing on funding for a proposed canal that
would run through Rankin's district and connect the Gulf
of Mexico with the Tennessee River, Truman wasn't much
interested. HST instructed White House aide Bill Hassett
after preparing the following reply to Rankin, "Bill: You
suggest a reply. Mine seems rather abrupt and a little too
diplomatic."*

[Early October 1949]

Dear John:

I read your telegram of October first with a great deal of
interest. I've been interested in the Tombigbee Canal for a
long time but the economy block, made up principally of
Dixiecrats and Southerners who have been against my program, have rather cooled me off on this subject. They are
extremely on the economy side when Social Legislation is up
but when it comes to "pork barrel," and this is a "pork barrel"
project, they are right in the front line with hats off and their
hands out.

I'll consider the Tombigbee project but I can make you no
promises on it.

Sincerely yours,

*The Korean War ended further consideration of the Fair
Deal. Then accusations that his administration was riddled
with corruption compounded Truman's troubles. Stories
about influence-peddling by government agency officials
filled the newsmagazines. "Natural Royal Pastel Stink," Time
labeled its story about how a White House stenographer had
been given a natural royal pastel mink coat by a friend of*

her husband's. Her husband had connections with the Reconstruction Finance Corporation, and the "friend" wanted low-interest RFC government loans for his business clients. This "RFC Mess," as Newsweek *called it, was investigated by a Senate subcommittee. While no illegalities were found, Truman haters had a field day bringing into question his honesty and the honesty of those who worked for him. The President confided to liberal Republican Senator Charles W. Tobey (whom Truman liked and who served on a Senate committee investigating organized crime) that if the truth were known, a lot of congressmen would go to jail for taking money from people whom they had helped obtain RFC loans. Tobey mulled the matter over, then wrote HST, "I have asked myself over and over again how we are justified in investigating crime on the part of individuals all over the country . . . while at the same time withholding from the subcommittee and the public the information which you said you had and would give me." The guilty, whether they be organized-crime mobsters or errant congressmen, deserved punishment, he said, and asked that the President give him the evidence.*

Truman wrote Tobey, but then did a little mulling himself and decided to file his letter. He telephoned the Senator instead.

March 27, 1951

Personal and Confidential

Dear Senator Tobey:

I read your letter of the twenty-sixth of March with a great deal of interest and, for your information, concrete evidence along the line which you suggest is almost impossible to obtain although it could be obtained if the same investigative procedures were used as have been used with regard to other persons investigated. I think you would find it almost impossible to do that.

The communications with which I am familiar are not in themselves incriminating documents although in my opinion they are unethical. These documents are in the files of the RFC and are available for the inspection of the Committee. My suggestion to you would be to go down to the RFC and take a look at the files and then use your own judgment.

As I said before I have no concrete evidence to give you and I don't think I implied that I had in our conversation. If I did, I did not intend to. Of course, you are exactly right about the ethics of the proposition that all parts of the population ought to be treated alike.

Sincerely yours,

Truman's opponents forced him to the wall during his last months in office over the question of who owned the submerged oil-rich lands on the continental shelf bordering California, Louisiana, and Texas. New technology had made offshore drilling possible, and oil companies, in concert with state officials, wanted state rather than federal ownership. Truman argued that that part of the continental shelf beyond the lowest tidemark belonged to the union at large. Several Supreme Court decisions had tilted toward federal ownership but left the final determination to Congress.

Texas, with her heritage of having once been an independent republic, pushed hard for a law deeding state ownership. Amon G. Carter, Fort Worth newspaper publisher, outlined for the President reasons why Texas deserved title to these "tidelands," including the fact that money to be derived from them was targeted for public schools. Referring to Carter during a speech to a liberal audience, Truman said, "I got a letter from a fellow in Texas today [sic], who is a friend of mine, and he was weeping over what the school children of Texas were going to lose if Texas didn't get its oil lands nine miles out from the shore. And I composed a letter to him, and then didn't send it."

April 25, 1952

Dear Amon:

I appreciate very much your letter of the seventeenth about the Tidelands situation.

I wonder if it ever occurred to you that the United States, as a whole, has a very deep interest in the general assets of the country as represented by the so-called Tidelands. You know my definition of Tidelands is "from high tide to low tide" — and I think that the States should have complete control of the land that is uncovered by the water when it is at low tide.

I have no doubt, however, that the United States Government, as a whole, owns all the mineral contents of the land to the continental shelf from low tide. The Supreme Court of the United States has made a decision on this subject and I don't think the Congress has any right, with the help of Dixiecrats and Republicans, to take those assets away from the country as a whole and if I can prevent it they are not going to do it.

Sincerely yours,

Harry S. Truman

P. S. I certainly appreciated the article about Margaret which appeared in your paper a few days ago. It was a grand article and pleased Mrs. Truman and myself no end.

Truman could not finally prevent Congress from granting "tidelands" ownership to the states, but he saw to it that the lawmakers would have to wait until Republican Dwight Eisenhower became President. He vetoed a submerged-lands bill awarding title, and for good measure, in what became a futile attempt to block further action, he declared the continental shelf a naval petroleum preserve four days before he left office. "I see no good reason for the Federal Government to make an outright gift, for the benefit of a few coastal States, of property interests worth billions of dollars — prop-

erty interests which belong to 155 million people," he had written in his veto message in May 1952.

This, plus a short note from the President, prompted Amon Carter to write Truman again. He protested the veto and challenged HST's explanation that his action had been motivated in part by a Supreme Court decision making the continental shelf vulnerable to foreign intrusion. If anything, Carter insisted, the court's ruling made state ownership even more necessary.

The chief executive, preparing to attend the 1952 Democratic National Convention (which would nominate Adlai Stevenson as the party's new standard bearer), wrote Carter a second unmailed letter.

June 21, 1952

Dear Mr. Carter:

I appreciated very much your good letter in further reference to the offshore oil deposits.

I, of course, am glad to have your views on the subject but I am still not convinced that the findings of the High Court are correct but when the Court makes a decision it is the law of the land. As President of the United States I shall endeavor to enforce it.

Sometime or other, when the country ceases to suffer from "electionitis" I'll be glad to sit down and have a conversation with you on many subjects.

Sincerely yours,
Harry S. Truman

Chapter 7

DEMOCRATS OR HIGH HATS?

Diary Entry
Saturday, October 29, 1949

. . . Just read an old editorial from the Globe-Democrat today which came from Roosevelt's files of 1940. They'd decided that Missouri had gone to hell because I'd beaten the double crosser Lloyd Stark for the nomination for the Senate![1] Stark had sent the piece to Roosevelt. It's hell how fate works. Stark wanted to be President — I didn't. Stark's buried politically because he is intellectually dishonest. I'm forced on the Democratic ticket as V.P. by the man who thought Stark was tops — and I'm the President and in my own right. . . .

Desk Note
August 12, 1952

The Governor of Illinois arrived at 12:40 P.M. His plane was 20 minutes late. We had pictures taken at my desk with

---

[1] While serving as Missouri governor, Stark entered the 1940 Democratic primary against Truman after pledging that he would not seek the candidacy for Truman's Senate seat.

Senator Sparkman behind us leaning over looking at a paper (which was my appointment list). Then we went back to the Cabinet Room. . . .

Everyone had a chance to say a word to Gov. Stevenson and Senator Sparkman. . . . I told the assemblage that our objective was to win the election, that I wanted to win as much as did the Governor. He said he thought that I was more anxious, if that were possible, than he was to win. Then I told them that I wanted my staff to give the Governor every possible help and cooperation, that I was ready to take orders, that the nominee of the Democratic Party was its head and that all of us must obey orders. The Governor expressed his appreciation, and we adjourned.

I took Mr. Stevenson and Mr. Sparkman into my private office and explained to them all the duties and obligations of the President. . . . We discussed campaign procedure, decided we'd both make Labor Day speeches and then that he would take the lead and make the issues and that I'd follow up in October and nail down the record. He would make the future program clear and we'd both wind up in a blaze across the nation.

Well we'll see!

Desk Note
December 28, 1962

I've just been informed that the Democratic Party of which I have been an active member since I was seventeen years old has gone high hat and is charging one thousand dollars for the privilege of sitting with the President of the United States [*John Kennedy*] at a dinner!

The President of the United States represents 180,000,000 people who have no other person to look after their interests. The President and the Vice President are the only elected public officials by the 180 million.

It is my opinion that ten thousand Democrats at five dollars apiece for the privilege of sitting with and seeing the President as his guest would be worth ten thousand times ten or one hundred times that to the Democratic Party. When the Party of the People goes high hat on a cost basis, it no longer represents the common every day man — who is the basis of the Democratic Party.

America's Democratic and Republican parties, unlike political parties in Europe, are not cemented together by fixed social and economic principles. Loosely organized and quarrelsome, the Democratic party especially reflects the country's regional, ethnic, and racial diversity, and during the postwar era many Democrats simply worked against the Democrat in the White House. Harry Truman, a realist in most regards, never fully accepted this reality about his political party. He considered it to be America's best hope for public leadership, believed its domestic mission was to defend against the high hats, and saw its true members as Jacksonian, little-"d" democrats like himself. "You know," he said, "I have known people who have had every honor that the Democratic Party can give them, and then when the Democratic Party needs them they will go out with the rich boys and see if they can't help themselves on the other side and let the Democratic Party go 'flooey.' I don't like it — I don't like it."

As an organization man, Truman believed in devotion and loyalty to the group. You stick together whether it be family, field-artillery battery, Tom Pendergast's political club, or the national Democratic party. Even after "Boss" Pendergast went to prison for paying gambling debts instead of his income taxes, Truman would not denounce him. When Tom died in early 1945, the newly sworn-in Vice-President defied critics and traveled home to Kansas City to attend Pendergast's funeral.

The following year, after Truman became President,

Kansas City's congressman, Democrat Roger C. Slaughter (whom Truman considered a high-hat Republican in disguise), stood for reelection and the White House received some disturbing news. It seemed that despite Truman's well-known desire for Slaughter to be defeated, Tom Pendergast's nephew Jim, the President's friend from World War I days, backed Slaughter's candidacy in the forthcoming Democratic primary. Feeling betrayed by striking labor-union leaders and now seemingly by Pendergast, HST penned Jim a letter that, together with its unused, torn-up envelope, surfaced thirty-four years later in Truman's personal papers.

May 17, 1946

My dear Jim:

I had hoped to be in Kansas City tomorrow and Sunday but Mr. Lewis, Mr. Whitney and Mr. Johnston[2] have prevented my leaving.

They are doing to me just what Mr. Slaughter has been doing to me in the Congress. I understand that you expect to support Mr. Slaughter in his throatcutting of the administration since I took over. I had never expected that to happen, because I have never believed loyalty to friends to be a one way street.

Lewis, Whitney, Johnston, Murray[3] and all other labor leaders made me certain promises when I took over. They all lied to me. Mr. Slaughter begged me with tears in his eyes when he came here to help him get on the House Rules Committee. I took him to Rayburn[4] and he promised by all he held holy he'd go along on administration matters.

The meanest Republican in the House could have done no worse. So you see he is in the same class with Lewis et al.

---

[2] Organized labor leaders John L. Lewis, Alexander F. Whitney, and Alvanley Johnston.
[3] Philip Murray, president of the Congress of Industrial Organizations.
[4] Representative Sam Rayburn, Speaker of the U.S. House of Representatives.

And *my* friend Pendergast is supporting him. I understand that this is so because of certain appointments to the military & naval schools.

I can't meet such competition as that, of course, being only a life long supporter of my friends at home and not a Rabbit.[5]

I'm only trying to say to you Jim that we will come to the parting of the ways if you humiliate me in my home county by supporting a cut throat like Slaughter.

Sincerely,
Harry

Rumors of Pendergast's betrayal proved unfounded, and Slaughter, confronted by a phalanx of opposition in the Democratic primary, lost to his Truman-backed opponent. But as another unmailed letter written half a decade later to James Pendergast demonstrates, neither HST nor his friends back home enjoyed continued good fortune in Kansas City politics. Results of a municipal election reached Truman in early 1951 during a presidential stay at the winter White House in Key West, Florida, and they elicited from him this melancholy undispatched response.

[Late March 1951]

Dear Jim:

I appreciated very much your letter. I did have a very good change of scenery at Key West but you can't call it much of a rest as I do just about as much work down there as I do at home, only I don't have the number of personal calls that I have here. The routine is just the same and after being there ten days it is just as tiresome there as it is here so I was just as anxious to come back as I was to go down there. I suppose that will last as long as I have the office.

---

5   Two factions, the "Rabbits" and the "Goats," vied for political power in Kansas City Democratic politics. Truman was a member of the latter faction, which was aligned with Pendergast.

I was very much disappointed in the result of the election in Kansas City and I still don't understand it. It certainly would be a fine thing if we could get Kansas City back into the picture once more as a progressive Democratic town. I don't think the so-called "clean-up" boys have made one step that has improved conditions of the city. It seems since they have been in power about all they do is kowtow to the Kansas City Star and then let the river take its course. It seems to me that the Kansas City spirit is dead, buried and forgotten. They would have a wonderful chance to get the Democratic Convention if they had any get-up and go about it. When I was Presiding Judge of the County Court we put on a Republican Convention which nominated Herbert Hoover — when I was sixteen years old I was page at the Democratic Convention which met there in 1900 and the city is in much better condition from a housing standpoint to take care of a convention now than it was in either one of those years but I suppose it is wishful thinking to dream of anything like that happening in the town under its present management.

I hope your family are all well.

Sincerely yours,

On the national level, Truman thought he headed up a cleansed, united, and forward-looking Democratic party after he beat Thomas E. Dewey in 1948. For one thing, he had won without the party's conservative Southern wing, the "Dixiecrats," who organized the States Rights party and ran Strom Thurmond as their presidential candidate. Republicans, not Democrats, suffered from sectionalism, Truman believed. But journalist Frank Kent editorialized otherwise, and in reply the President wrote Kent an unmailed letter.

March 5, 1950

My dear Mr. Kent:

I've been reading the Sunday Washington Star. Your revival of the Republican Party is most interesting. Nothing in the world would please me more than a real revival of the G.O.P. It won't happen though unless the people are concerned that the leadership of the Republican Party have a program.

You know, of course, that the G.O.P., to start with, was a sectional party. Until it ceases to be a sectional party it can't win.

What I was trying to prove and did prove in 1948 was that the Democratic Party is a national party. We won without New York, Pennsylvania, New Jersey and the industrial east. We won without the "solid south." We won as the party of the people as a whole — farmers, laborers, small business men — and even some big business men. Now why?

You say 25% did not vote. Therefore we won on a minority. If the 25% had voted it would have been a landslide. You and your columnist friends, along with the pollsters, had convinced some six or seven million people that there was no reason to go to the polls! Remarkable! Isn't it? or Wasn't it?

People no longer in this great country can be fooled by people who write for money. Nor can they be misled by such busy editors and managers as Hearst, McCormick, Roy Roberts and old man Gannett.

I fear very much that the band wagon has long ago passed you and Mark Sullivan[6] by. In my youth both of you were flaming liberals. Now you are in the Grover Cleveland, John Garner[7] class. You are living in 1888. Too bad. We need

---

[6] Noted turn-of-the-century author, who wrote a contemporary history of the United States.

[7] Franklin Roosevelt's first Vice-President.

your brain power to meet 1950 situations. I wish Ponce de Leon had been successful — we'd still have you and Mark as liberal democrats.

While his unmailed missive to Frank Kent didn't touch upon it, by March of 1950 Truman had become alarmed over an extremist faction within the Republican Party. "I am in the midst of the most terrible struggle any President ever had," he wrote his cousin, General Ralph Truman. "A pathological liar from Wisconsin and a block headed undertaker from Nebraska[8] are trying to ruin the bipartisan foreign policy. Stalin never had two better allies in this country. I must make an effort to stop that procedure."

"That procedure," however, was not stopped during Truman's presidency. Indeed, it soon became known as "McCarthyism" in reference to tactics used by Wisconsin Republican U.S. Senator Joseph R. McCarthy, in his mushrooming crusade to root out Reds from government, who he claimed were entrenched within the Truman Administration.

Shortly after McCarthy first warned of the alleged internal menace in a February 1950 Wheeling, West Virginia, speech, he sent Truman a wire reiterating his claim that fifty-seven Communists worked within the U.S. State Department. The President's reply to McCarthy reposes today in the Truman Library with a line drawn across it, marked in Truman's hand "File."

[February 11, 1950]

My dear Senator:

I read your telegram of February eleventh from Reno, Nevada with a great deal of interest and this is the first time in my experience, and I was ten years in the Senate, that I

---

[8]   The President's reference is to Republican U.S. Senators Joseph R. McCarthy (Wisc.) and Kenneth S. Wherry (Neb.).

ever heard of a Senator trying to discredit his own officials. Your telegram is not only not true and an insolent approach to a situation that should have been worked out between man and man but it shows conclusively that you are not even fit to have a hand in the operation of the Government of the United States.

I am very sure that the people of Wisconsin are extremely sorry that they are represented by a person who has as little sense of responsibility as you have.

Sincerely yours,

Nevertheless, McCarthy's political influence increased. After the 1950 congressional elections, the President, while acknowledging a letter from former Roosevelt "Brain Truster" Rexford Guy Tugwell, expressed but did not send his opinion of McCarthy's campaign tactics during that election.

[December 12, 1950]

Dear Mr. Tugwell:

I can't tell you how much I appreciated your good letter of December seventh.

It is necessary, of course, that we forget the lies and vicious attacks that were made in the last campaign. Very few of the statements made against the administration in the campaign were based on facts. The McCarthy attacks on the State Department and the people outside the State Department were a fabrication of lies out of the whole cloth but it didn't help the country any. I hope that that sort of thing will stop and that we can get together and meet the conditions as we find them. I am sure that can be done.

The McCarthy era bracketed the last three years of Truman's presidency and the first two of Eisenhower's. The senator's downfall came in late 1954 after nationally televised congressional hearings showed a scowling Joe McCarthy attack the United States Army for "shielding Communists." Soon McCarthy's Senate colleagues had censured him for behavior unbecoming a United States Senator, and by the end of the Eisenhower years national hysteria had subsided.

In 1961, in keeping with the new era of good feelings, the Bolton Lake, Connecticut, chapter of the extreme right-wing Webster Quimmly Society experienced a change of heart. Its leader wired Harry Truman, "WE DO NOT BELIEVE YOU ARE A COMMUNIST." *Truman snapped back:*

[Late September 1961]

Why don't you believe it? It has taken you a long time to find out.

Too bad.

H.S.T.

"Send it collect," he instructed Rose Conway. Then, with resignation, HST scratched that out and scribbled, "Just file it."

In addition to crossing swords with the McCarthyites, Truman expended much of his presidential energy trying to maintain harmony within the ranks of his own political party. A letter he did not send to Vice-President Alben Barkley (he talked to him instead) demonstrates the lengths HST had to go to placate the Democratic Party faithful at the grass-roots level.

May 27, 1950

Dear Alben:

John Cashmore[9] was in to see me yesterday and discussed with me the possibility of your going to New York for a Sunday School Convention. I promised John I would mention it to you — that is what I am doing.

---

9   President of the Borough of Brooklyn.

I know you are burdened, as much as I am, with requests to go places but John is one organization Democrat, who is an honorable man — how he does it I don't know. He is a Protestant and his District is made up of Catholics and Jews. You have to give a man good who can stay at the top and do that.

You do as you like about the request that he makes.

I hope everything is going well with you.

Sincerely yours,
Harry

New York state politics especially attracted Truman's attention in 1950. Republican Thomas E. Dewey, HST's defeated foe two years before, sought election to a third term as New York's governor, and Truman hoped Dewey might be replaced by a liberal Democrat. Dewey won reelection, however, in part because of conflict between urban and rural factions within the state's Democratic ranks. As this unmailed letter to New York Democratic chairman Paul E. Fitzpatrick reveals, the President considered injecting his hand into the state's intra-party fracas. Fear that his intervention might further aggravate the situation probably kept Truman from mailing it.

June 28, 1950

Dear Paul:

I've written to Ed Flynn and Cashmore[10] suggesting that you, Flynn and Cashmore, along with the head of Tammany Hall should get together and try to work out a program for the election of a Democratic Governor in New York.

If something isn't done promptly in this situation we will be faced with the same program as we were in 1942 and 1948.

---

10 These letters were also withheld.

If you think a conference in my office might be helpful, I'll be glad to see you, Flynn and Cashmore any time you want to come down.

Sincerely yours,

His last year in office, Truman was reminded that involving himself in his home state's political scene might also cause embarrassment. Stuart Symington, who had served as Reconstruction Finance Corporation director, entered that year's Missouri Democratic primary contest for the party's U.S. senatorial nomination, and Symington wrote the President about his campaign strategy, including the fact that the state's country newspapers had come out for him. Truman answered Symington but withheld his letter because he decided to support Symington's primary opponent, Missouri's Attorney General, J. E. "Buck" Taylor. After Taylor lost to Symington in the Democratic primary, Truman probably wished he had mailed this letter.

May 12, 1952

Dear Stu:

I appreciated very much your good letter of May sixth. Sometime when I am in the neighborhood or when you are close to Washington I'll be glad to see and talk with you.

That address at Paris [*Missouri*] was a good one.

No man can run for the Senate in the coming campaign unless he runs on the record of the democratic Administration from 1932 to 1953. It is hard for some politicians to understand that just because a few newspapers throw bricks at the Administration that they will gain by picking up the bricks and re-throwing them.

In my political experience when I was running for United States Senator, Vice President and President I always had

the Metropolitan press against me and I never would want
to run on the Democratic ticket unless they were doing
everything they could do to cut my throat.

Sincerely yours,

*One Missourian not running for office in 1952 was Harry
Truman; he had confided his retirement plans to his staff in
November 1951. Chief contenders for the Democratic presidential nomination were Tennessee Senator Estes Kefauver
(whom Truman hated) and Illinois Governor Adlai Stevenson (whom Truman tolerated). Left no choice at the party's
Chicago convention, the President helped Stevenson become
the Democrat's standard bearer.*

*On the Republican side, bets were that anti–Fair Deal,
"Mr. Republican" of the United States Senate, Robert Taft,
would get the GOP nod — that is, until General of the Army
Dwight D. Eisenhower turned to politics. Taft, like Truman,
ended up on the outside looking in during the presidential
campaign. A Herblock cartoon in the Washington Post
showed a lonely Bob Taft on vacation with hand cupped to
his ear asking, "Any Calls For Me To Go Whistle-Stopping?"
The cartoon stirred in Truman feelings of kinship toward
the conservative Republican, and he almost sent him this
letter.*

August 15, 1952

Dear Bob:

I noticed the enclosed cartoon in the Washington Post
this morning and I rather felt like I had company in a condition which I am sure neither one of us anticipated.

If the amateurs in command of your party organization
follow the same program as the amateurs in control of mine
you and I will have a grand time as spectators. I've never
yet seen uniformed people in control of political affairs who

really knew what to do. I am certain that you and I could give our Party organizations some very good advice if they are willing to take it.

Sincerely yours,

An intellectual in speech and manner, Adlai Stevenson earned the epithet "egghead" during the presidential campaign. His strategy was to tack to the country's conservative tide, keeping as far distant from Truman and his floundering Fair Deal domestic program as possible. Claims of corruption within the Democratic administration in Washington especially troubled the Illinois governor, and he triggered an unmailed Truman spasm when he responded, however obliquely, to an Oregon newspaper's query about "the mess in Washington."

[Mid-August 1952]

My dear Governor:

Your letter to Oregon is a surprising document. It makes the campaign rather ridiculous. It seems to me that the Presidential Nominee and his running-mate are trying to beat the Democratic President instead of the Republicans and the General of the Army who heads their ticket.

There is no mess in Washington except the sabotage press in the nature of Bertie McCormick's Times-Herald and the anemic Roy Howard's snotty little News.

The Dixiecrats and the Taft Republicans along with Nixon, Knowland, Harry Byrd and the seniority chairmen of the Key Committees of the House and the Senate make the only mess in the national scene.

You seem to be running on their record and not on the forward looking record of the Democratic Administration as represented by the President, the Vice President and the Speaker of the House.

I've come to the conclusion that if you want to run against

your friends, they should retire from the scene and let you do it.

When you say that you are indebted to no one for your nomination, that makes nice reading in the sabotage press, but gets you no votes because it isn't true.

There are more votes on "skid row" than there are on the "North Shore" for the "Party of the People." New York, Illinois, Missouri, California, Ohio and the farm belt are worth more to you than Texas and the Dixiecrat States.

You fired and balled up the Democratic Committee Organization that I've been creating over the last four years.

I'm telling you to take your crackpots, your high socialites with their noses in the air, run your campaign and win if you can. Cowfever [*Kefauver*] could not have treated me any more shabbily than have you.

Had I not come to Chicago when I did, [Kefauver] the squirrel headed coonskin cap man from old man Crump's State,[11] who has no sense of honor, would have been the nominee.

Best of luck to you from a bystander who has become disinterested.

No more had Truman calmed down and filed away this blast than both the governor and his running mate, Senator John Sparkman, jabbed further insults. Sparkman, a political moderate from Alabama, worked hard to woo old-line Southern Democrats back to the party fold, and he quickly alienated the President. First, he sent Truman an open letter urging release of a government oil-investigation report. More serious, the Alabaman also granted an interview to U.S. News and World Report wherein he criticized Truman's handling of the steel strike that spring. As for Stevenson, he

---

11   Reference is to Tennessee, whose other U.S. Senator was Edward H. Crump.

quietly declined HST's private invitation to discuss joint campaign strategy. When reporters needled the President as to when he might meet with the governor, Truman insisted, "If he wants to see me, I will be glad to see him; and if I want to see him, he will be glad to see me. We are in perfect agreement." Two unmailed letters spoke otherwise.

[Late August 1952]

My dear Senator Sparkman:

I've just been reading the reports of your spasm in the sheet run by that old counterfeit Dave Lawrence on the steel strike.

Why didn't you come to the man who knows for your facts? Why didn't you obtain those facts and state them from the platform — the Democratic platform — instead of in an interview in a rotten Republican Propaganda Sheet?

This is your second effort to offend the President of the United States by a bone head approach.

You and Adlai seem to be running against the President and the Administration instead of the Republicans and Eisenhower. Your open letter to me on the oil cartel would have been unnecessary had you come to me for the facts.

Only Brewster, Bridges, Williams and Noland write letters to the President in the newspapers.[12] You've joined them! I wonder whether you understand that when you pull bone head plays like this you create glee and happiness in the camp of Ike and his cohorts.

You are receiving thanks and praise from the great metropolitan dailies for kicking the only friend who can cause your election, just as he caused the nomination of both you and Stevenson. I want no publicity or credit for my part in the Convention. But too many people know the facts for history to be garbled by any fool approach by the candidates now.

---

[12]   Republican Senators Owen Brewster, Styles Bridges, John J. Williams, and William F. Knowland.

I can enjoy myself in a rocking chair on the famous balcony if that's what the Democratic Nominees want.

[Late August 1952]

Dear Governor:

I have come to the conclusion that you are embarrassed by having the President of the United States in your corner in this campaign.

Therefore I shall remain silent and stay in Washington until Nov. 4.

You understand that I had decided in 1949 that I would not be a candidate for this greatest office in the history of the world, again.

In January 1952 you came to the Blair House at my request and we discussed a successor to me in the White House.

You were coy and backward, advancing various reasons why you had to be the candidate for Governor of Illinois, your divorce, your belief that you did not have the qualifications, etc.

Again a month later we had the same sort of a discussion.

When the time for the Democratic Convention approached I sent the Chairman of the Democratic Committee to see you. Frank McKinney was the ablest chairman the Democratic Committee had produced in my recollection. You stalled and gave him the same answer you had given me.

Then I called the Vice President to the White House along with Mr. McKinney and a number of other able national politicos and told him that we would support him for the nomination for President.

You of course know the rest of the story. Barkley became discouraged and withdrew. He was intending to leave Chicago a whipped man. I called Mr. McKinney and Barkley's farewell speech was the result.

On Friday morning you called me and told me that your friends — among them the Governor of Indiana, who is now running on the Republican ticket[13] — wanted to nominate you. You wanted to know if I would be embarrassed by that procedure. I told you that I would be highly pleased.

That afternoon I boarded a plane and landed in Chicago in the middle of the afternoon. The Convention had recessed with no nomination. Kefauver had some 360 votes, you had 330 odd, and favorite sons had the balance.

I sent one of my aides to see Mr. Harriman, one to see Gov. Dever of Mass., one to see the Minnesota and the Michigan delegations with instructions to switch to you. Harriman and Gov. Dever switched, the amateurs didn't until later.

You were nominated and you made a grand acceptance speech.

Then you proceeded to break up the Democratic Committee, which I had spent years in organizing, you called in the former mayor of Louisville [*Wilson Wyatt*] as your personal chairman and fired [*Frank*] McKinney, the best chairman of the National Committee in my recollection.

Since the Convention you have treated the President as a liability. You brought in Beardsley Ruml[14] as finance chairman, who is in the Wilson Wyatt class as an amateur. You had your Chicago lawyer made chairman of the National Committee. He is a fine man but has no political contacts and is completely ignored by both you and Wyatt.

But — I can't stand snub after snub by you and Mr. Wyatt.

When the President after much thought (from a political point of view, which may be beneath *high level* consideration) asks the Democratic Candidate to come to a strategy conference and is coldly turned down and referred to a crack-

---

[13]   Henry F. Schricker, a conservative Democrat, whom Truman accused of aping the Republican line in his current campaign for the U.S. Senate.
[14]   Businessman associated with R. H. Macy and Company.

pot, it seems to me that the Democratic Candidate is above associating with the lowly President of the United States.

I shall go to the dedication of the Hungry Horse Dam in Montana, make a public power speech, get in a plane and come back to Washington and stay there.

You and Wilson can now run your campaign without interference or advice.

Again Truman backpedaled. He whistle-stopped for the Democratic ticket coast to coast in October, although in many of his "give 'em hell" speeches he sounded as though he rather than Stevenson was running against Ike. In one speech he accused Eisenhower of deserting his former boss, General George C. Marshall, by endorsing fellow Republicans, such as Joseph McCarthy, who had called Marshall a traitor. Truman also hit hard at Ike's running mate, Richard Nixon, especially after he heard that Nixon had called him a traitor. The Republican national committee's chairman offered HST $1,000 if he could prove that Nixon had really called him a traitor during the campaign. Truman proved it to his own satisfaction but not to the Republican's, so the money was never paid.

Baltimore insurance man Martin A. Fitzpatrick wrote Truman after he left office that whether Nixon had said that or not, it was certain that most public officials put the country's welfare behind their own selfish partisan interests. Truman's reply, found in a folder labeled "Richard Nixon," contained the notation "Drafted but not Mailed."

[Late February 1956]

Dear Mr. Fitzpatrick:

I was rather surprised and a little shocked by your attitude toward the public officials who are elected to run our country.

You might just as well have made the same statements

about the members of the Continental Congress who passed the Declaration of Independence or about those men who met in 1787 to write the Constitution of the United States.

It is almost too obvious that your opinion of public servants has been formed by the writings of such publishers as the Pattersons, the McCormicks and the Hearsts, who have aroused unfounded bitterness against our national political leaders for more than a hundred years.

In 1864 the Chicago Tribune printed the full text of Lincoln's speech at Gettysburg with the comment that the President had made the "usual ass of himself." Believe me, it is flattering to be put in such company.

I know a Fitzpatrick in St. Louis whose viewpoint is quite different from yours, and he draws some of the finest political cartoons to be found in the United States.

Sincerely yours,

Another unmailed "Nixon letter" was found in Truman's desk after he died. W. L. Harriman of Detroit wired that HST's insults regarding Nixon "MAY TRANSFORM REPUBLICAN ELEPHANT INTO SQUIRREL HEAD BUT MAY ALSO PROVE DEMOCRATIC DONKEY TO BE THE SAME OLD ASS." *They might, Harriman said, cause many Democrats to become Republicans.*

[Late November 1958]

L. A. [*sic*] Harriman . . .

Your nice wire was appreciated. None was received when Squirrel Head Nixon called the former President a traitor. Did you wire Jenner of Indiana when he called General George C. Marshall a traitor with the approval of Wisconsin's McCarthy?

Old line Republicans love character assassins. They are not assets to free government. Character assassins can not be insulted. If you love them vote the Republican ticket.

Harry S. Truman

After Ike beat Stevenson by over six million votes in 1952, Truman, in an unmailed letter to Washington Post publisher, Philip Graham, listed his reasons why Stevenson lost.

December 15, 1952

Dear Mr. Graham:

I appreciated very much your letter of December eleventh. The last campaign was one of the most vicious that I ever witnessed and I've been actively engaged in them for forty years. The attitude of the Scripps Howard Papers, the Hearst Papers and the vicious attacks that were made on the President by Governor Dewey and by the Republican candidate for President were unprecedented. Of course, I can't take them "lying down." Your own publication has had some vicious editorials since election not founded on fact. There is one this morning.

The South and the Bible Belt were both flooded with propaganda sheets that were really unprintable and they were put out at the request and expense of the Republican Committee. There was not a single Metropolitan newspaper, except the Cox papers, that was editorally favorable to the continuance of the most prosperous Administration in the history of the United States. Why, I could never understand. I suppose it was the pressure of the advertisers.

The National Association of Manufacturers and the National Chamber of Commerce have been doing everything possible to sabotage the anti-inflation machinery which has been working very successfully for the last year and a half. The economic situation as reported by the Council of Economic Advisers and the independent committee working on economics is sound.

I sincerely hope that Ike will have a successful Administration and you can rest assured that I expect to do nothing to cause him worry or embarrassment on my own part. It is hard for me to stand for "flub-dub" though, which is intended to fool people who are worried about their sons and daughters in action.

Sincerely yours,

Dejected and headed for private life following Ike's victory, Truman decided to cancel a scheduled appearance at Chicago's Roosevelt College. The regrets, however, were sent in a different form from this original.

November 17, 1952

Dear Doctor Burnette:

I've been thinking about the appearance at Roosevelt College, and have come to the conclusion that it will not be the proper thing for me to make appearances for some time after the new Administration takes over.

I have decided to go to Independence, Missouri and stay there for the time being unless it becomes absolutely necessary for me to make a statement to head off a misrepresentation of the facts.

I regret very much that I will not be able to be with you for the Roosevelt College affair. Maybe I can do it at some later date.

Sincerely yours,
Harry S. Truman

Truman went home, but he did not retire. Though he was in his seventies by the end of Eisenhower's first term, he carried on as though he were thirty. After four years of Ike, the Missourian itched to help defeat him in 1956. He was not, however, happy over the prospect that Senator Estes Kefauver might become the Democratic Party's presidential candidate that year. As in 1952, Kefauver competed with Adlai Stevenson for the Democratic nomination, and Truman, convinced that Kefauver had purposely embarrassed him while Truman was President (the Senator had launched a well-publicized national crime probe in Kansas City), judged "Mr. Cow Fever of Tennessee" to be "ignorant of history, an amateur in politics and intellectually dishonest."

Although worded far more judiciously than in his other, more private, expletives on Kefauver, Truman decided to file away this first impulsive draft of a response to J. Joseph Donahue's request that he support Kefauver in the 1956 Democratic convention.

July 23, 1956

Dear Jiggs:

Your letter of the 13th was very much appreciated, and I think we can work things out satisfactorily at the Chicago convention.

I am sorry that my admiration for the Senator from Tennessee is not the highest, but my experience with him while I was President was disappointing. If he is now sincere in his professions of a genuine interest in the general welfare of the country, I think that you and I can show him the way to be helpful, but he will have to demonstrate his attitude by action.

I'll talk to you further the first time I see you. I expect to arrive in Chicago on the 9th of August and will stay at the Blackstone Hotel until the convention is over.

Sincerely yours,

The convention gave Stevenson a second try against Eisenhower and chose Kefauver as his running mate. A loyal Democrat to the end, Truman campaigned for the party's ticket. After hearing him give a campaign speech, an Illinois mortician wrote the former President that he was "pitting class against class," and recommended that Truman drop out of politics. HST withheld this reaction to the undertaker's complaint.

September 6, 1956

Dear Mr. Gauss:

I can appreciate your interest in the burial of a citizen of the United States. As far as I am concerned, however, I still believe in free speech, and I hope to continue to say what I please for a long time to come.

If you read enough of my utterances, perhaps you might find something in them to your advantage.

Sincerely yours,

During the campaign, Look *magazine ran a story "Tragic Fact: Our Young Voters Don't Care," which cited a survey indicating that only two out of five college students eligible to vote would do so that November. The magazine's editor, Jack Squire, wanted Truman's comment. He never received it.*

September 18, 1956

Dear Jack:

The article in Look is curiously interesting. It seems to show that the youngsters are thinking for themselves and that they have little respect for pollsters. I wouldn't answer you either!

When they reach the stage of responsibility, I am certain that their decisions will be in the public interest.

Sincerely,
Harry S. Truman

But voters in November again chose the amiable Ike, although at the same time they elected a Democratic Congress. Eisenhower's reelection stung Truman. Among other things, he still smarted over the former general's behavior toward him four years before on Inauguration Day in January 1953. Defying custom, Ike as President-elect had declined to lunch with the outgoing President, and had added further insult

when he complained to Truman en route to his inauguration
that HST had embarrassed him by ordering his son John
home from Korea to attend the ceremony.
Shortly after Eisenhower won a second term in 1956,
Truman penned him an unmailed "congratulatory" message.

November 28, 1956
My dear Ike:
You are elected again and this time without a Congress of
your own choosing. A record with only one precedent, back
a hundred and eight years ago — 1848 when old Zach Tay-
lor another professional General was elected with Millard
Fillmore, who was the Know Nothing Candidate in 1856.
Your V. P. [*Nixon*] is not that far advanced.

I sincerely hope you'll wear a homburg hat and a short
coat as you did in 1953 at the inauguration. You'll no doubt
have your son present, as you should, but you won't have to
scold me for having him there. You can now order him to
be present yourself.

I am sincerely hoping you'll pray as loudly and as long as
you did in 1953 — Jan. 20th. I also hope you'll go to Egypt
and Palistine [*sic*] and perhaps to Hungary and Poland in
order to surrender to the Kremlin as you did in Korea in
1953.

With Eastland, Thurmond, Talmadge, Holland, Byrd and
McClellan,[15] you should be able to really inaugurate your so
called New Republicanism.

By all means consult Lausche of Ohio, Revercomb of
W. Virginia and your two boys from old Kentuck.[16] With
that crew you should be able to wreck T.V.A., give away
the balance of our national resources, completely ruin our
foreign policy and set the country back to 1896 and 1929.

---

[15] Pro-Eisenhower Southern Democrats in the Senate.
[16] Just-elected Eisenhower senatorial allies, Republicans John Sherman
Cooper and Thruston B. Morton.

Best of luck and may the honest Democrats and Liberal Republicans save you from disaster.

"My only objective," Truman wrote Charlie Murphy later, "is to save the Democratic Party as the party of the people, the people who have no pull at the seat of the mighty." With Ike unable to run for a third time in 1960, Democratic prospects looked brighter, but HST fretted beforehand over factionalism within his party. Various groups maneuvered for advantage in the forthcoming election. Angered by what appeared to be a power play by Democratic national chairman, Paul Butler, Truman wrote, then tucked away, a letter to his friend, House Speaker Sam Rayburn.

July 8, 1959

Dear Sam:

I noticed that Paul Butler is also "firing from the hip," without any consultation with Democrats that count.

I don't like it and I know that you are as unappreciative as I am. It seems to me that when the time comes to lay out the Convention next year some of us should get together and pick out the keynote speaker and the presiding officers of the Convention.

I want Sam Rayburn to preside and I'd like very much to have a keynote man who can put the Democrats on top of the election and then let the nominations take the regular course and end up with two men on the ticket who can lead us to victory.

I've no ax to grind, only the welfare of the United States of America and the Democratic Party. They are synonymous.

Sincerely,

Harry

John Kennedy was not Truman's choice for Democratic nominee. He was too young, too Ivy League, too rich, too

Catholic. "Senator, are you certain that you are quite ready for the country or that the country is ready for you in the role as President in January 1961?" the old sage asked at a surprise news conference. Stuart Symington, by now seasoned as a U.S. Senator from Missouri, became Truman's choice.

Expressing his disenchantment with the Democratic Party's eastern wing while attending a political confab in Washington, the former President snapped that fortunately the party was durable enough to tolerate its "synthetic liberals." Joseph Clark, who had been present at the gathering, was upset by Truman's remark and later wrote him to ask him to explain it. The Missourian's explanation, however, ended up in his desk drawer.

January 31, 1960

Dear Joe:

I found your long hand letter in the piled up mail when I returned from Washington.

The Democratic Party has been the only political party since 1808 that has had the ordinary man's interest in its concept of what government is for. That has been true through Jackson, Lincoln (who coined the phrase "Of, by and for the people"), Grover Cleveland in his first term, Teddy Roosevelt, to some extent, Woodrow Wilson and Franklin Roosevelt (without reservation).

I'll never forget 1948 when these so called "liberals" (synthetics I call them) went off the reservation and gave New York to Dewey. I came to the conclusion that they would rather have a man in the White House at whom a brick could be thrown than to have one who knew where he was going and why.

You and I are not going to fall out because of a small difference of opinion as to what's best for this great nation.

If these so called "liberals" do what was done in 1948

we'll have that greatest of great synthetic liberals, the Hon. Richard Nixon for President. Do you want him? Of course you don't.

Sincerely,
Harry

Our admiration is mutual

That rich old man, Joe Kennedy, had "bought" the Democratic nomination for his son, Truman charged as Democrats gathered in Los Angeles to select their candidate in the summer of 1960. Disgusted, he abruptly cancelled plans to attend the convention. After Kennedy got the nomination, Truman turned to history for solace and penned another unmailed letter, this time to Dean Acheson.

August 26, 1960

Dear Dean:

Your letters of the 12th and the 23rd really gave me the lift I needed. I have been as blue as indigo since the California meeting in L.A. It was a travesty on National Conventions. Ed Pauley organized it and then Kennedy's pa kicked him out! Ed didn't consult me!

That Convention should have been helped immensely if it had been in Chicago, St. Louis or Philadelphia. But it wasn't held at any of those places. You and I are stuck with the necessity of taking the worst of two evils or none at all. So — I'm taking the *immature* Democrat as the best of the two. Nixon is impossible.[17] So, there we are.

When I took the stand I did I hoped to help — but it didn't. I look at history and the period after Madison and then the one after Jackson. After Jackson we had Martin

---

[17] "He is a dangerous man. Never has there been one like him so close to the Presidency," Truman wrote Acheson later.

Van Buren, a smart fixer, and then William Henry Harrison, a "stuffed shirt" who insisted on riding a white horse to the Capitol — and a month later John Tyler was President. You know that old devil, who was my great grandmother's uncle, had some ideas of honor. He resigned from the Senate when he was not able to support Jackson's financial policy. Then came James K. Polk, a great President. Said what he intended to do and did it. Then three months after leaving the White House, went home and died!

Then old Zach Taylor came along, father-in-law of Jefferson Davis. He became famous at the Battle of Buena Vista by telling Captain Bragg to "give them a little more grape." Winfield Scott "Old Fuss & Feathers" was as anxious as Grant and Ike to be President. Old Zach kept him out. But he ran again and was ingloriously defeated by one of his Brigadier Generals, Franklin Pierce — who always had the stomach ache or a pain in the neck when there was a shooting engagement in Mexico.

Franklin Pierce agreed to the repeal of the Missouri Compromise and signed the Kansas Nebraska Bill. With John Brown and his murders on the border between Missouri and Kansas these events caused the War Between the States — now officially called the Civil War, as was the War of the Roses in England.

I'm afraid I'm boring you but that is not the intention. I'm afraid that this immature boy who was responsible for picking out five great Senators may not know any more about the Presidency that he will occupy than he did about the great Senators. Only one, Henry Clay, belonged in the list. I sent him a list of a dozen or so but it wasn't used.[18] So, what the hell, you and I will take it and not like it but hope for the future.

---

[18]   Reference is to John Kennedy's book *Profiles in Courage* (New York: Harper, 1956).

Truman's fears subsided once Kennedy took office. Indeed, a few months before the young President was assassinated, he dictated a defense of JFK's performance. The letter was not dispatched to J. Neely Peacock, Jr., on advice of a Truman aide.

September 5, 1963

Dear Mr. Peacock:

I read your letter of August 31st, with a lot of interest and some surprise. You must remember that the Democratic Party has been through all sorts of conditions and in the long run it always emerged as the "Party of the People."

It is still the Party of the People and from your letter I judged you were a little prejudiced against the present occupant of the White House. He is a good Boston Democrat and, as happens with Presidents, the first years of his admintration he has had all sorts of paper wads thrown at him. If I were you, I would wait a while and see what happens.

That happened to Grover Cleveland during his first administration — but during his second administration he didn't receive a word of criticism because he was on the side of the special interest, even though he did not do as good a job.

Sincerely yours,

Nineteen hundred sixty-two was the last year the former President campaigned actively. His choice for U.S. Senator from Missouri that year faced an opponent whose father was a wealthy Kansas City banker and whose family had switched from Democrat to Republican. In a vindictive mood, Truman wrote, then filed away, a complaint to Rufus Crosby Kemper, senior member of the family.

September 5, 1962

Dear Crosby:

I have just been reliably informed that you have been putting pressure on and making threats to some of my good friends regarding the campaigns in the state of Missouri, particularly the one for the Senate.

Now Crosby, I don't like that sort of thing. In one instance you have ruined the political prospects of one of our good young democrats, by threatening to take his living away from him. You've got him working for a "Republican Kemper." That is something out of this world to me. Your father was my friend and the greatest part of his fortune came about because he was National Democratic Committeeman for thirty or forty years.

He was beaten for Mayor when he should have been elected. Your present friends the K. C. Star lied him into defeat.

Remember the Mexico & Orient deal when the Jackson County Democrats came to his rescue. I was there and I know.

Now I don't care a damn if one of the third generation of Kempers wants to go wrong because of the immense wealth of the family, but I do care if the second generation makes financial pressure a part of the campaign.

I have some forty thousand dollars in one account in your bank. I have twenty five or thirty thousand in a Library account and I have forty thousand in your brother's bank. Do you want me to do what you did to my young friend? I can cut you both off now and for the future if I want to. And Mo. will have two Democratic Senators.

Harry S. Truman

Chapter 8

HARRY TRUMAN,
HISTORIAN

Diary Entry
May 14, 1934

Tomorrow — today rather, it is 4 A.M. — I am to make the most momentous announcement of my life. I have come to the place [*as a candidate for the United States Senate*] where all men strive to be at my age and I thought two weeks ago that retirement on a virtual pension in some minor county office was all that was in store for me.

When I was a very young man, nine or ten years old, my mother gave me four large books called Heroes of History. The volumes were classified as "Soldiers and Sailors," "Statesmen and Sages," and two others which I forget now. I spent most of my time reading those books, Abbott's Lives and my mother's big Bible. . . .

In reading the lives of great men, I found that the first victory they won was over themselves and their carnal urges. Self-discipline with all of them came first. I found that most of the really great ones never thought they were great, some of them did. I admired Cincinnatus, Hannibal, Cyrus the

Great, Gustavus Adolphus of Sweden, Washington and Lee, Stonewall Jackson and J. E. B. Stuart. Of all the military heroes Hannibal and Lee were to my mind the best because while they won every battle they lost the war, due to crazy politicians in both instances, but they were still the great Captains of History. . . .

Desk Note
[1950s]

Readers of good books, particularly books of biography and history, are preparing themselves for leadership. Not all readers become leaders. But all leaders must be readers. Many readers become historians & teachers. They are retiring, timid when publicity is involved and are among the greatest assets to this republic.

Political leaders like publicity. It does them little good unless the historical background is there to support the publicity. No one ever loses by reading history, great literature — and even newspapers.

Herbert Hoover enjoyed the trout stream, Franklin Roosevelt the swimming pool, Ike the golf course. Harry Truman's recreation was a stack of books. Not too much fiction, though. He preferred accounts of people and places, human challenges and their deliberate or accidental resolution. Have a decision to make? Look to history, Truman believed, and you'll find a blueprint for action.

At sixteen, Martha Truman's boy Harry had already decided that most everything human beings experience had happened before — sometime, somewhere. His high-school theme books look like a present-day college honor student's, with world-history lecture notes neatly organized and detailed, English compositions that speak of duty, honesty, loyalty, and courage. History proved, young Truman argued in one, that the person who chooses security above risk in life exposes himself to deep trouble.[1]

Risk was something the Trumans had plenty of in 1901, the year Harry graduated from high school. His jack-of-all-trades father lost both their Independence home and their farm out near Grandview, and the family moved to Kansas City. A half century later, as thirty-third President of the United States, Truman, who had worked at various jobs in Kansas City, described in his longest and most richly detailed unmailed letter some of what he had experienced in that bustling beef-packing town. The letter was intended for Kansas City Star *editor Roy Roberts. The* Star *celebrated its seventieth year in 1950 with a fat tabloid edition, and the President concluded that the newspaper's ability to report history was about on par with its political acumen.*

June 12, 1950

Dear Roy:

I have been going through my centennial edition. It is most interesting. I wish you'd had someone talk to me about some of the events mentioned and some of the pictures displayed. At the top of the funnies you show the junction, 9th, Main and Delaware. Ninth Street was double track, Main, north bound and Delaware, south bound.

Independence Ave. cars were green, you have that right. 9th St. cars were red, and made connection with the "Dummy Line" which went to Independence. The crossing watchman to whom you refer in this picture once pulled my mother back from the curb in front of the C. & A. office and when she turned on him to tell him off he said "only saving your

---

[1]   These theme books, thought destroyed or lost, are in the possession of the President's niece Martha Ann Swoyer, who graciously allowed me to examine them.

life madam, only saving your life." He was too, for he pulled her back in time to miss a westbound car. We, of course, wanted to go east.

I also casually notice an article about John Wornall. My father was named for him because he was a great Baptist. My father was also named for his Uncle John Truman who, also, was a great Baptist.

I noted your article about 3rd & Campbell Sts. My Aunt Laura lived at 3rd and Campbell. She was voted the most beautiful girl in Jackson County and awarded the prize, but as is usual in such cases there was a protest. She gave the prize back to the judges and she was again given it unanimously. Her married name was Mrs. W. B. Eberhart. Two of her daughters are still living, and will confirm what I'm saying.

Again, at 9th & Main and Delaware just north of the C. & A. office was the Soda Fountain and Candy Shop of Jesse James, Jr. I was a pupil at Spalding's Commercial College in the New York Life Bldg. in 1901 and early 1902, studying debit and credit and Pitman Shorthand. Carfare and a quarter for lunch was all I received when I left home. I also took a music lesson from Mrs. E. C. White on these trips.

Well on one occasion I stopped in Jesse's place and had an Ice cream Soda — 5 cents. When I'd finished it — I found I had no nickle only a car ticket home. Jesse said, "Oh that's all right, pay when you come in again." I paid the nickle the next day! My father stood for honesty.

I don't like to be critical, but as you say in your editorials, there are a lot of misstatements and inaccuracies. My Grandmother Young saw the flood of 1844 and we took her to see the flood of 1903. Her comment was, "This flood is no greater, but more property is destroyed." She was a grand old Kentuckian and she had red hair!

And now Roy, I'm going to tell you something that's good for your soul. Your former boss Old Bill Nelson in my book is lower than the belly of a snake!

He prevented the proper development of Jackson County by two of his copperhead approaches and he was a copperhead in Indiana.

When he turned Washington Park into a cemetery instead of a grand residence addition, and when he split the city in the center with his Union Station, he ruined Jackson County as far as he could. Tom Pendergast was a gentleman alongside him.

He left an "Art Gallery" to make his peace with God Almighty just as Nobel and Rockefeller did but I don't think he fooled Jehovah — and you can't either. The characters you've ruined and the people you've made unhappy have more chance of being right with God than have old Pigfaced Bill Nelson, Nobel and John D. I only hope that the great forgiving God will be more charitable than I would be.

Sincerely,
Harry S. Truman

President of the United States in spite of you, Bertie McCormick and Willie Hearst.

[Warmed to his subject, the President continued.]

Of course, Roy, your century edition cares not for your number one citizen's contribution. No mention in your whole edition of the most convenient and efficient Court House in the county, no mention of the Andrew Jackson Statue by the greatest sculptor of our time, no mention of the planned road connections to the County and to Kansas, no mention of the attempted interstate plan which would make the region the greatest in the country. To do this you'd have to give a little, backward county judge and a knownothing U.S. Senator from Missouri some mention. He wants no mention from your lousy sheet! History will tell the tale and you and Big Pigfaced Bill won't even be mentioned.

Ain't it hell for a prophet to be without honor in his own home county, where he made his reputation that caused him to be Senator twice, Vice President and President in *his own right* of this Republic?

Roy, you also talk of the Air Age striking Kansas City. Well it struck and your boss Pigface Bill, old Bill Kemper and Henry Ford kept Kansas City from being the air capital of the world. That is why Karl Klemm committed suicide. Kansas City should have been the center of air manufacturing instead of Detroit. But old Kemper and Pig Face Bill Nelson prevented it — for a compensation. When I am no longer president of the U. S. I expect to set down a lot of facts that will be believed because people know I tell the truth and you do not.

Your writer talks of the theaters in Kansas City — and the old Grand is not mentioned. The Grand and the old Orpheum on west 9th Street with the old blood and thunder Gilliss were all we had from 1900 until the Willis Wood was built.

The Four Cohans, Primrose and Dockstader, Williams and Walker, East Lynne, Chauncey Olcott all came to the Grand.

Marguerita Sylva, Sarah Bernhardt, Eddie Foy, Chic Sale, and numerous other of the great vaudeville stars came to the old 9th Street Orpheum. Why didn't you ask someone who knows?

You've never mentioned the Great Weber & Fields appearance in Convention Hall with Lillian Russell at her best, Nat Wills and all the other great of burlesque.

As for Kansas City's musical taste — nothing is said. There was Parsifal, Lohengrin, Cavelleria Rusticana, I. Pagliacci, Les Huguenots, all by the Met. Opera in Convention Hall.

There was [*Ignace Jan*] Paderewski, who taught me how to play his famous minuet, [*Moriz*] Rosenthal, Augusta Cotlow, and the greatest of them all Josef Lhevinne, who came to Convention Hall. And Vladimir de Pachmann, and all those named above who came to the Shubert. There were Donald Brian, Joseph Cawthorne and two other stars in the Girl from Utah famous for the song "They'll Never Believe Me." Marlow[*e*] and Sothern in the "Taming of the Shrew." The Spring Maid, a lovely musical show and many others.

Richard Mansfield at the Willis Wood in Dr. Jekyll & Mr. Hyde. I was afraid to go home after seeing it. Walker Whiteside in Richard III, Sir Henry Irving and Ellen Terry in The Merchant of Venice, Julius Caesar and Hamlet.

Then there was the old Woodward Stock Company at the Auditorium. They played Hamlet, Romeo & Juliet, Midsummer Night's Dream, and again at the Shubert Robert [*Bruce*] Mantell in Richelieu.

So you see you have talked to me. But an ignorant country boy from Grandview.

"Your Kansas City history is about as accurate as your daily columns from Washington," Truman told Roy Roberts in a much abbreviated, less vituperative letter. Roberts answered that under present world conditions (war had just broken out in Korea), such matters were unimportant, that "the President of the United States should not be vexed with such things."

A few months later, as the President pondered the Communist attack upon South Korea and our efforts there and in Europe to contain Communist expansion, he ruminated over ancient history. After all, everything mankind experiences has happened before — sometime, somewhere. He decided that our resistance to communism's spread was no different from the Greeks' stopping the Persians in the fourth century B.C., the Franks' stopping the Moslems at the Battle of

Tours in 732 A.D., and the Swedes' containing Tsarist Russia during the time of Peter the Great. America was taking its turn in defense of Western civilization against "the [E]astern hordes." A letter Truman received from former Roosevelt justice department official Norman Littell triggered off this undispatched lecture on world history.

[Mid-September 1950]

Dear Mr. Littell:

Bill handed me your letter.

For your information I am somewhat familiar with the historic incident to which you refer and that is one reason that I've been trying my best to contain the "eastern hordes" as represented by Russia at the present time. One of the main difficulties is the fact that Russia started to come out of the dark ages in 1917 — by 1930 she had started back and is still on the way back to the time of Genghis Khan and Tamerlane.

You overlooked the fact that Charles Martel's action took place at Tours. Also John Hunyadi made a great stand at Belgrade against the Turks. The Moors were already half-way across France when they met Charles at Tours and were turned back. The son of Charles Martel[2] is partly the cause of a lot of modern strife in Europe. He divided his kingdom between his sons and created the split between France and Germany, which has never been healed. King Henry IV of France had the remedy,[3] but he was assassinated before he could act.

Sweden at the height of its glory was the barrier to the eastern horde but the growth of the German and Austrian empires placed Sweden in the background. The Swedes have never again come back to their proper place in world affairs.

---

[2] Reference is actually made to Martel's grandson, Charles the Great.
[3] "The Grand Design," considered a forerunner of the League of Nations.

Finland, Norway, Britain and Turkey are the only people left who will fight for their homes and firesides whether they have guns or sticks and stones. Our objective, of course, is to revive that fighting spirit of all Europe and see if we can't impress the Russians so we will be in a position to get peace in the world. That is all I am trying for — world peace. We want a lasting peace. We have no designs on any country. We want to see countries happy and prosperous.

Referring to the Athenians in the battle at Marathon in 409 B.C.,[4] don't forget Xerxes and his attempt to accomplish the same purpose. The great Darius to whom you refer was the greatest of all Eastern Monarchs, in my opinion. But he lost his standing in the world when he tried to conquer the Slavs, just as did Napoleon and Hitler.

I am more than happy to receive communications from you on any subject. I enjoy also "showing off" my historical bent to one who'll read it.

Sincerely yours,

As for American history, Truman was a Civil War buff. After he left Washington, it was a favorite topic of conversation between him and Bob Weatherford, his hometown's mayor. Knowing of the former President's interest, Columbia Records executive Goddard Lieberson sent him a newly released album that contained songs of the Confederacy. Rose Conway wrote on HST's acknowledgment, "The President said to hold."

[Late January 1955]

Dear Mr. Lieberson:

I certainly appreciated "The Confederacy." I immediately listened to it and enjoyed it immensely. I remember my mother sang those songs when I was growing up.

---

[4]   The battle actually occurred in 490 B.C.

I was highly amused by your story about Lee. I once told Harry Byrd[5] I expected to write a book on the white trash of Virginia and what became of them. I had a man who worked for me on the farm from Grayson County, Virginia and he said to me one time that he thought there ought to be a lot of good people in Virginia because all the white trash had been emptied into Ohio, Kentucky and Indiana. I told that story to Harry Byrd one time and he didn't think it was funny.

The facts are that the so-called trash are usually the ancestors of our really great men. The ancestor worshipers who stayed in England, France and Spain did not make the Western Hemisphere great. It was the so called lower classes who wanted to improve their lot who made North & South America and Australia and New Zealand great.

The Lords, Ladies, Counts, Earls and Dukes still have their descendants in the old countries but when something has to be done for their salvation a man "south of the tracks" has to do it, as Pershing and Eisenhower did!

H.S.T.

The man from Independence, who counted himself among those commoners "south of the tracks," believed also that through the years his Democratic Party had proved its worth. Republican Seward F. Sanford of Seneca Falls, New York, thought otherwise and said so in a letter he sent Truman at Christmastime 1954. Where did liberalism of the Democratic Party stripe end, and socialism begin? Sanford asked. He also contended that before the Democrats found they could blame Herbert Hoover for America's economic problems, they had been "the party of world free trade and business depression."

That last accusation did it. Truman, out of office two

---

5   Democratic U.S. Senator from Virginia.

years and angered over what he considered Republican give-
aways to big business under Eisenhower (like the Tidelands
Oil Bill), drafted Sanford an unmailed treatise on recent
American political history.

                                    [Mid-December 1954]
Dear Mr. Sanford:

I was highly intrigued with your letter of the twelfth, particularly the second paragraph. Of course, the Democrats
have always been for the free exchange of goods and services
between the countries of the world but when you charge the
Democrats with business depression I want to call your attention to a little history.

The great panic after the Civil War which came in 1872
was engineered under General Grant.

The next great panic of 1892 was the result of the Benjamin Harrison administration.

The next money panic of 1907 was after the full dinner
pail of William McKinley and Theodore Roosevelt and the
top notch of them all came after eight years of Republican
rule in 1929.

I can't for the life of me see how Democrats could be
charged with business depressions, all of which have happened under Republican administrations and most of which
were straightened out by following Democratic administrations.

The Democratic policies and programs were outlined by
Woodrow Wilson in his messages to Congress and in his policies pursued while he was President in his first term as most
of the great reforms came during that term — the Federal
Reserve and Federal Trade Commission being the outstanding ones.

Then after the twelve famous years of Republican "business prosperity" from 1921 to 1933 the Democrats came
along, revised the Federal Reserve Act to bring it up to date,

saved the banks, pulled the country out of the hole and put it in a position where the distribution of income was as nearly fair as it could be made under the circumstances.

You will find also that the so-called conservative program to which you refer is a program of special interests. It has been amply demonstrated just recently when the assets of all the people have been given to promoters and private interests.

I wish you would study the history of the country beginning with George Washington and take that history, administration by administration; and then it would do you a lot of good just to refresh your memory on affairs beginning more recently in 1896. It will enlighten you considerably on what public service really means and what the welfare of the country really is.

I hope you have a Merry Christmas too and from a good Democrat. You brought this situation on yourself!

Sincerely yours,

Truman came home from the presidency nearly broke. A pension for former chief executives was still in the talking stage. Nor did he receive help at first to maintain an office and a staff; he even had to buy postage stamps for the piles of mail he sent out each week. Impressive job offers came from big corporations. Truman considered them publicity stunts and turned them down. He would not lend his name for promotion — the presidency was not for sale.

For the man on the street, however, the former President paused willingly to pen autographs, pose for pictures, and sign and return photos of himself for those who wrote requesting them. One request, from Mississippian Hugh C. Ellis, especially amused him. Ellis wrote that a friend had bet that he couldn't get Harry Truman's personally autographed picture to hang in his newly decorated office. Truman, reminded of a joke that circulated in the 1920s about "Silent Cal" (President Calvin Coolidge, known as a man of few words), decided to oblige Ellis with the picture and for good measure dictated Ellis a personal reply. However, Ellis lost his bet because, when Miss Conway gave the President the typed, ready-to-mail letter, Truman noticed on Ellis' return address that he was a tire company's public relations director. *Truman refused to sign.*

December 6, 1954

Dear Mr. Ellis:

I am not going to treat you as President Coolidge treated the young lady who sat by him at dinner. She tried all evening to get him into a conversation and all she could get was — yes or no or a grunt. She finally told him that she had made a bet that she could get him to say more than three words during the dinner. He merely said to her — "You lose."

Hope you don't lose the bet.

Sincerely yours,

Writing his memoirs topped HST's list of priorities after he left the White House. He needed the money, but even more importantly, he wanted to print "the facts" before the "sabotage press" distorted his role in history. "You know," he told lawyer-friend Sam Rosenman, "if it weren't for the misrepresentations that have been made about President Roosevelt and about his successor in office I'd never have tried to tell the facts." "What I am trying to do," he wrote Dean Acheson, ". . . is tell the truth and the facts in a manner that people can understand and in my own language."

But Kansas City writer Webster Schott, who had tried unsuccessfully to interview Truman about his memoirs project, later wrote that writing HST's memoirs had been a group effort. Schott stressed in a Kansas City Star *column that the former President had been aided by a string of collaborators, including professional researchers and writers. Schott's story elicited another unmailed Truman missive aimed at* Star *publister, Roy Roberts.*

March 24, 1956

Dear Roy:

I notice on the editorial page this morning a lot of hooey by a gentleman by the name of Webster Schott.

He has tried time and again to get into my office on a gossip basis and he has never been able to make it.

I am sorry that you saw fit to publish his article.

Sincerely yours,

An unmailed handwritten letter found in the former President's desk (there were twelve in all) describes how, after heading up a Senate committee investigating war production costs, Truman became Franklin Roosevelt's vice-presidential running mate in 1944, and then President when Roosevelt died nine months later. "Bill," to whom the letter is written, remains unknown, the only addressee among those in this book who couldn't be identified.

October 31, 1959

Dear Bill:

Your letter of Oct. 26th touched a cord that will never be forgotten by me.

I want you to know, and those interested to know, that I tried in every way possible at Chicago in 1944 to prevent my nomination for the Vice-Presidency. My career up to that time had been in the Senate. The Committee, of which I was chairman, had spent its time trying to help the president win the war, by keeping the conditions behind the fighting lines as they should be. It appears that was accomplished, because those who had been most disturbed by that Committee's work finally admitted that it had contributed to efficiency and had saved the taxpayers fifteen billions of dollars. While that was not a great deal of saving in a 600 billion expenditure, it was something, and there were very few investigations by Senate and House Committees afterward.

After World War I, there were 116 investigations which contributed nothing to the winning of World War I.

During the War Between the States (Civil War to the Yankees), there was a Joint Committee on the conduct of the war. Senator Chandler of Michigan was Chairman, Ben Wade of Ohio, President Protem of the Senate — who wanted Andrew Johnson convicted on his impeachment so he could be president — and Congressman Gooch from Massachusetts, were on that most unpatriotic committee.

It is my impression that Douglas Freeman made the statement that the Committee on the Conduct of the War was worth two divisions to General Robert E. Lee.

After Gettysburg, that Committee had General George Meade before them, and abused him as if he were a pickpocket. By luck or guidance in history, [I,] the Chairman of the Committee to Investigate the National Defense Program, was acquainted with what might happen in a war if a Senate or Joint Committee interfered with its conduct.

That committee had no reports from the [*opposition*] minority.

This is a preliminary statement to give you a reason why I was nominated for Vice-President in 1944.

When Mrs. Truman, Margaret and I were on the point of leaving Independence for Chicago on Friday before the convention of 1944, a phone call came from Washington. It was the Hon. James Byrnes. He asked me to nominate him for Vice-President. He informed me that President Roosevelt had endorsed him. I told him if Roosevelt had endorsed him, I'd be glad to do what he asked.

Before I could reach the car, the phone rang again, and Senator [Alben] Barkley asked me to nominate him. I told him of my conversation with Jimmy Byrnes.

Went to Chicago and found no one for Byrnes or Barkley. Was finally forced into the nomination by the president [*telephoning*] from San Diego. He'd never told *me* what he wanted!

[*Roosevelt, looking gaunt and ill at the 1945 inauguration, died three months later.*]

When the expected happened, I was on my way to Sam Rayburn's office on the House side of the Capitol. When I arrived, Speaker Rayburn told me that Steve Early wanted me to call him back at the White House.

I called him, and he said, "I wish you would come to the White House right away and come in at the Pennsylvania Avenue front door. Come up to Mrs. Roosevelt's parlor on the second floor."

I supposed that the President was in Washington for Bishop Adkin's (of the Episcopal Church) funeral. Roosevelt was an honorary pall bearer.

Mrs. Roosevelt told me of the President's death a short time before I'd had the call from Steve Early.

I called a Cabinet meeting and notified all the official family to come to the Cabinet Room and at 7:09 P.M., April 12, 1945, I was sworn in as President of the United States.

The first decision was to go ahead with the United Nations program in San Francisco.

From that time on, it was decision after decision: Rehabilitation of Europe (Marshall Plan), Greece and Turkey, Berlin Air Lift, Trieste, Iran's Evacuation, Korea.

You know the rest. Hope this answers your question.

Sincerely,

Harry S. Truman

Before leaving public office, Truman had begun plans to build a library to hold his papers and to allow students to study the history he had made. He considered putting the archives on land he owned jointly with brother Vivian and sister Mary Jane in Grandview. The University of Missouri and Kansas City also offered construction sites. "Bob, I've got to make a decision and I've got to make it in two weeks," he told Bob Weatherford. "I've got to decide where I'm going to put this library." "Well," the Independence mayor said, "why don't we put it right here at home where it belongs?"

Weatherford took the two weeks to negotiate use of a hilltop park on the north side of town for the library. Successful, he drove Mr. Truman the five blocks from the Truman home to the park site. The former President stood silent among the trees for a moment, gazed at the Kansas City skyline in the distance, and declared, "Bob this is great! This is what I wanted. Right here will do it. This is the place." Getting back into the mayor's Buick, Truman unknowingly punctuated his decision by slamming the car door on Weatherford's finger! The President never learned about it. The mayor, injured but elated, wrapped his bloodied finger hastily in a handkerchief and drove Truman home before seeking medical attention.

Contributions for the Truman Library's construction came from every quarter. An anonymous offering from Ohio read, "Dear Sir: Enclosed you will find one dollar bill, honestly earned, my donation for the establishment of your library. I am glad you are happy with your family. You look so happy in your pictures. May God keep you that way." A little girl sent fifty cents in dimes. The President instructed that she be awarded a certificate reserved previously for big contributors. "This fifty cents to her is probably more than $5,000 by comparison," he said. Independence civic clubs *held auctions, the town's police force raised $484.25 by playing basketball astride donkeys, union artisans volunteered their labor, and Truman himself spoke at fund-raising dinners across America.*

While he was recuperating from gall-bladder surgery in mid-1954, about the time the money-raising campaign gained momentum, Truman set on paper some thoughts about the future. Why this letter, intended for successful library fund-raiser Abe Fineberg, remained unsent is a mystery.

[September 1954]

Dear Abe:

Charlie Murphy has just been out here for a visit. He told me, among other things, that he is going to be helping the Democratic National Committee raise some money, which they need very badly. Charlie says frankly that he knows nothing about how to raise money but he is going to try it. I told him to get in touch with you and I thought you could give him some help, and I know you will.

I've been thinking a lot in recent days about the Library and particularly how much you have done to make it possible. I can never repay you or thank you enough, but you know I appreciate it. I'm looking forward now to having the Library in Independence.

It looked for a while like I might not be around to see it built, but I'm recovering well now. I think I'll be here for quite a while to look after the Library, and pay my respects to the Republicans, and engage in other good works.

Sincerely,

Once the Library was built, an educational fund was established to encourage research there and donations were solicited. Stanley E. Whiteway of Secane, Pennsylvania, wrote Truman that he had included a donation in his will, prompting a handwritten response from the former President. But then HST instructed his secretary to thank Whiteway, and his own letter went into a desk drawer.

January 21, 1959

My dear Mr. Whiteway:

When I came to the office this morning at 8 A.M., through a blizzard that should have stayed in North Dakota, I found your wonderful letter which had been brought out to the Library special delivery.

Your statement about leaving something to the institution hit me where I live. It is my ambition to make the Library a center for the study of the Presidency. That great office has been neglected and misrepresented by so-called historians. It is the greatest executive office in the history of the world. I say that not because I held it but because I became acquainted with it by experience. I had read everything on it before fate passed it on to me. This Republic of ours is unique in the history of government and if the young people coming along in the future generations do not understand it and appreciate what they have it will go the way of the Judges of Israel, the City of Greece, the great Roman Republic and the Dutch Republic.

These young people must understand that our great Government was obtained by "blood, sweat and tears" and a thousand years of effort on the part of the great thinkers over that period and blood-letting revolutions and sacrifices by the people. Why, we even had to spend four bloody years whipping ourselves to make the Constitution work. And we are still at it — trying to make it work!

Sam Rayburn has set up an institution at Bonham, Texas, which is the history of the Legislative branch of the Government from the first Continental Congress. The Chief Justice has succeeded in obtaining the approval of Congress for the use of the $300,000.00 which Mr. Justice Holmes left to the government, to write definitive biographies of the 88 Justices of the Supreme Court.

You see what I have in mind. A real history of the World's Greatest Government from the real sources.

Your contribution will go to the educational fund which will be set up to furnish scholarships for high school youngsters interested in government. I'll probably be in the past sure enough when your will is probated because I'm 74½ now but still "going good."

Thanks for your good letter. You see what you got yourself in for!

One Library fund-raising project angered Truman. Accustomed to greeting famous performers such as Jimmy Durante and Jack Benny at the Library, HST got his "Missouri up" when he came across an invitation sent out by Dr. Philip C. Brooks, the Library's director. According to the invitation, Jose Iturbi would perform in concert to benefit the Truman Library Institute's student grant-in-aid program, and a donation was requested from those seeking tickets. Not consulted beforehand, and feeling shunted aside by Doctor Brooks and the director's academic-type friends, the President wrote but then withheld this complaint.

February 25, 1963

Dear Dr. Brooks:

So there will be no misunderstanding, Iturbi is coming to the Library to give a concert for me at his own invitation, and that concert is not one in which a money-raising proposition was to be considered.

It was due to the fact that I was incapacitated on account of an operation that matters were taken over and the situation started to be used as a promotion affair. It is not a promotion affair and that idea of sending out invitations and asking people for $25.00 a piece is completely out of line with what I, as the honoree of Iturbi, expected to do. As many as are necessary will be invited to come free and those who pay their money will have to stand outside if they can't get in.

Sincerely yours,

From his office located in the Library's back wing, Truman frequently sauntered up front to the museum section. "Let's go out and visit the customers and walk through the museum," he would tell Milton Perry, curator in charge. When VIPs visited him, Truman gave them what he called "my twenty-five-cent tour." Pictures and paintings, a reproduction of his White House oval office, bejeweled gifts from royalty, a piano, dishes, and historical relics from his White House years: he had given them all to the American people.

Not everyone, however, applauded the museum's trappings. Mrs. Robert T. Foley, upon learning that an original White House mantel had been installed in one of the display rooms, wrote Truman that she was shocked "that a former President has removed objects belonging to the White House — installing them in his own personal monument." She asked that he return the original and enclosed in her letter a picture of the mantel in question. Truman, sensitive to any suggestions that the Library served as a monument to himself and convinced that Mrs. Foley had erred in her accusation, labored over two drafts of a reply. He finally gave up and instructed, "Just file it."

[Early December 1961]

Dear Mrs. Foley:

I was more than happy to receive your note regarding the mantel in the State Dining Room in the White House.

The Mantel in the picture, which you sent me, has long ago been destroyed, and I am sorry that is the case. The original one was in the White House when John Adams lived there, and when Mrs. Adams used the East Room to hang out and dry her washing!

I have a picture of the mantel that was left there by me. I don't know who changed it, or where they got the idea of putting in that funny-looking thing that is there now.

The mantel I have in the Library would not, under any circumstances, fit the situation. It is twice too big for the present location. The mantel that was there when I left, and of which I have a picture in my Library, was a most beautiful Adams marble mantel and, under no circumstances, would I have had it destroyed.

You will have to get in touch with somebody else to see what became of the mantel I left there.

Sincerely yours,

Missouri artist Thomas Hart Benton, renowned for his panoramic portrayals of life in mid-America, had painted a mural in the 1930s for Missouri's state capitol that Truman detested. In the mural's lower righthand corner, representing the state's big-city life, Benton had included a bawdy Kansas City scene complete with cigar-wielding Tom Pendergast. Understandably, Truman, when asked to appear at Benton's studio upon completion of a giant Benton painting, "The Kentuckian," penned an unmailed critique of the artist's work.

January 7, 1955

Mr. Bernstein:

Your letter of Jan. 6: In the first place I know nothing about ART with a capital A, particularly the frustrated brand known as Modern.

I don't like Mr. Benton's Kentuckian. It looks like no resident or emigrant from that great State that I've ever seen. Both of my grandfathers were from Kentucky as were both of my grandmothers. All of the four had brothers and sisters most of whom I saw when I was a child. They did not look like that long necked monstrosity of Mr. Thomas Hart Benton's.

I won't encourage him to do any more horrors like those in Missouri's beautiful capitol.

H.S.T.

Once Truman met Thomas Hart Benton, he changed his mind. Crusty and cantankerous like the former President, Benton became friends with Truman, and by 1961 a colorful Benton mural depicting Independence as the historic gateway to the Santa Fe Trail graced the entryway to the Truman Library.

HST decided the next things the Library needed were portraits of all the former Presidents. A friend commissioned a Japanese artist to paint copies of famous presidential paintings, but before the project got underway Benton objected to having the copies made exactly like the original paintings. Referring to his mural, Benton wrote Truman that he had "a four hundred and ninety five square foot interest in the appearance of the Truman Library," and he urged that only the faces in the famous presidential paintings be copied and that the portraits be made uniform in size. HST held back his reply to Benton and went ahead with the original plan.

January 17, 1964

Dear Tom:

I appreciated your letter of the 9th, and your suggestion.

My whole idea was to get together a set of the pictures of the Presidents as they appear in the White House for the education of the youngsters who come here to look at them. But the people who spell art with a capital "A" do not think it is a good idea.

I would be glad to talk to you about it and your suggestion about having the heads of the portraits arranged in such a way so as not to offend the people who spell art with a capital "A".

Sincerely yours,

While Independence's first citizen felt understandable pride in the library on the hill, he insisted that it was not his personal monument. "They call it 'the Truman Library' but it isn't my Library — it is an archives building . . . ," he wrote a friend. When given the news that a poll taken among seventy-five historians had ranked him among the greatest of American Presidents, he remarked, "You know when monuments or positions in history are assigned to men who are still walking around changes may have to be made and the monuments destroyed! You can never tell what they may do before getting into that pine box six feet underground."

But Truman reacted with less good humor when a Look *magazine article assigned him a prominent place in recent history. Sent a prepublication copy of "A Quarter Century: Its Human Triumphs" (wherein black major-league baseball star Jackie Robinson, scientist Albert Einstein, and he were judged mid-twentieth-century champions over adversity), Truman addressed his evaluation of the story to* Look *editor Richard Grande. "Just file it," he later penned across the letter's bottom. "We won't mail it. Pegler and Sokolsky couldn't have been meaner in a sarcastic way."*

November 21, 1961

Dear Mr. Grande:

I read the so-called favorable article which you proposed to publish under the name of Catherine Drinker Bowen. It is a rather "snotty" article under the headline that it is favorable.

I would much rather it would be written as an attack on
the subject than to have it appear as a usual-Time-Life-Look
approach to what they look upon as favorable approach.

Sincerely yours,

*During his later years, Truman most enjoyed talking with
young people about American history, especially about the
presidency. He toured college campuses, and at the Library
told museum curator Milton Perry, "When you get groups
of kids coming in, put them in the auditorium and come get
me." It didn't matter, he said, if he had somebody on the
phone or in his office, "because there's nothing I'm doing
that's more important than talking to these kids." He answered their questions and usually made a pitch about how
important it was to learn "all the facts" about an historical
event.*

*The old President-turned-historian gave the same advice
without success to* This Week *editor William I. Nichols.
Nichols' magazine planned to run an excerpt from a new book
on America's World War I doughboys. Included was to be an
episode describing Captain Harry Truman's participation in
the 1918 Meuse-Argonne offensive. Would the President
care to comment? Nichols asked. Truman wrote Nichols
that the battlefield account was inaccurate, that it contained
"very few facts," and to remedy that situation sent the editor
an abstract from his memoirs. Nichols answered with an
apology that it was "much too late" to make changes in the
forthcoming excerpt. He said that while he was sorry that
the book's author had used faulty documentation, he was
not sorry the magazine had chosen to publish it, "for [he was]
sure that the millions of people who read* This Week *will be
warmed by this glimpse of the commander of Battery D in
action."*

After reading his boss's intended reply to Nichols, a Truman aide advised: "This letter is trouble!" and urged that it be held. Here is a composite of the pigeonholed letter's first two drafts:

July 18, 1963

Dear Mr. Nichols:

Your letter of July 11 was quite a surprise to me. I have always known that Time and This Week cared very little for the facts and the truth — but I have been charitable because I labored under the misapprehension that perhaps — perhaps you couldn't find the truth and the facts.

You've confessed that you don't want the facts.

I have a lecture course that has been given in sixty or seventy colleges and universities from Maine to Southern California and from Washington State to Key West, Florida.

I have spoken to 300,000 or 400,000 students and in all probability will lecture to twice that many in the next two and a half years. I have from 200 to 400 youngsters in the Library auditorium every week from March 1st to Nov. 15th.

I shall use your letter as a theme on the reliability of slick magazines — and there is nothing you can do about it. What I'm hoping is that you'll try to stop me from telling the truth about you who have never told it about me!

Sincerely (not very),

By the time HST returned to Independence in 1953, that postwar technological marvel, television, had moved from the furniture-store window into nearly everybody's living room. The former President soon recognized the new medium's educational potential, but he winced when CBS president Merle S. Jones asked him to approve a TV dramatization of a historic moment during his White House years. The matter concerned a scene depicting him as President (played by an actor viewed from behind) awarding the Congressional Medal of Honor to Lieutenant Thomas J. Hudner (played by another actor). Because an adviser agreed to look into it, HST's answer to Jones went into the files.

July 29, 1955

Dear Mr. Jones:

In reply to yours of the 15th, I don't believe in fake Medal of Honor Presentations. I consider the presentations of those Medals of Honor — and I presented more than all the Presidents put together — was one of the most important of the functions which I rendered while I was President of the United States.

There is nothing in the world equal to the Citations for those Medals of Honor and I certainly wouldn't approve of anything that would in any way make a travesty of that ceremony. I don't see how it can be worked out on a fake basis without that happening.

Sincerely yours,

In the early sixties, independent TV producer David Susskind wagered that the real *Harry Truman would appeal to television audiences. He spent $200,000 to film two one-hour pilots of a projected documentary series featuring the former President himself commenting on major events during his presidency. When the TV networks showed no interest in the series, Susskind bowed out.*

Novelist Merle Miller, who had worked as the series scriptwriter, committed to paper what he knew about the real *Harry Truman after talking with and observing him during the filming of the two pilots. Miller sent HST a thirty-six-page typed manuscript titled "Truman," which, with some modification, became part of his bestselling book,* Plain Speaking, *published the year after Truman died. In a letter to HST accompanying his essay, Miller informed the former President, "The piece has now been sold to* The Saturday Evening Post," *adding that he hoped he liked it.*

Truman didn't like it. Neither did California retired public-relations executive David Noyes, who handled HST's literary dealings. On Truman's behalf, Noyes got agreement from the Post *not to publish Merle Miller's recollections. As for Miller, he never knew that the* real *Harry Truman had written him an unmailed letter.*

April 25, 1963

Dear Mr. Miller:

I thank you for sending me the article which you proposed for the Saturday Evening Post.

I am not in favor of such articles, especially this one which has so many misstatements of fact in it. I am sorry that is the case and if you publish it I shall make that statement public.

Sincerely yours,

The television networks gave various reasons for not buying the David Susskind–produced series, none of which Truman believed. He wrote NBC's Robert Kintner: "Old man Sarnoff [Kintner's boss, RCA president David Sarnoff] . . . is not very fond of me. In fact, he headed off a historical program that I was going to put on but I am going to put it on in spite of him and I will appreciate it if you will tell him that."

Several years later, Truman got a chance (he thought) to turn tables on television's top brass. Asked by NBC to participate in a program on Andrew Jackson, Truman declined and considered for a time sending producer James Nelson this explanation for his refusal. After he wrote this letter, Screen Gems, the production firm that replaced Susskind, also failed to sell the documentary series.

January 22, 1964

Dear Mr. Nelson:

I am under contract with Screen Gems for a series of articles on what happened during my administration and one of those series has to do with Andrew Jackson.

I don't know whether you remember it or not but when we tried to get you to take a hand in the making of the articles which we are working on with Screen Gems, you had other things to think about and couldn't even consider it.

The same thing was true with CBS, but now you are both trying to get me to do films that are a violation against the contract I have already made. Both of you had a chance but you didn't take it.

Sincerely yours,

At about the time television attracted Truman's interest as a vehicle with which to disseminate historical knowledge, John Kennedy used it to become President. Had it not been for the televised debates between him and his opponent, Vice-President Richard Nixon, during that 1960 campaign, the far-better-known Nixon would have won. Of course, Kennedy's campaign strategists employed other, more traditional, means to win a national following for the young senator from Massachusetts. One was the pamphlet Kennedy or Nixon: Does It Make Any Difference? *written by award-winning Harvard historian Arthur Schlesinger, Jr., well known for his multi-volume account of Franklin Roosevelt's first years as President, and for other important historical works.*

Schlesinger's publisher sent the pamphlet to Independence, and it stirred in Truman memories of past political battles against Republicans and that "sabotage press." As he reflected about Franklin Roosevelt, it especially tickled him that because FDR had won four presidential terms, the Republicans, together with the Dixiecrats, had sponsored the twenty-second amendment to the Constitution, which limited presidential terms: now, a decade later, it prevented Eisenhower from running again. But memories aside and partisan though he was, the old self-taught historian decided that the "Hawvad Doctor" could benefit from a little instruction. His handwritten note to Schlesinger, though typed up by his secretary, was never completed and mailed.

[Mid-September 1960]

Dear Doctor Schlesinger,

I have just finished your pamphlet entitled "Kennedy or Nixon." I find it a most interesting dissertation.

Your entirely objective and unbiased approach to the life and background of the Vice-President intrigues me no end. I can only wish you had been as "objective" and "unbiased" in the Senator's life and background.

Your sly remarks about Franklin Roosevelt's eggheads is great. You of course know that most of them deserted him when he needed them most. The Beards[6] and Rex Tugwell have virtually accused him of treason.

Naturally the Republicans of the 80th Congress and the Democratic States that voted for and tied the 22nd Amendment to the Constitution are now weeping salt and crocodile tears because they did it. None of them I'm sure had even read the debates of the Constitutional Convention of 1787 on the subject. I hope you have read them.

There is another great document on the subject of "higher" education which I'm sure will interest you. That is President Buchanan's veto message of the first Land Grant College Bill. If he were alive today he no doubt would appreciate no end your dissertation on politicians and vote getters.

---

6   Historians Charles and Mary Beard.

My definition of a politician is a man who understands "Government" and who knows how to make it work. The metropolitan "free press" is a publisher's and an advertiser's press as are the slick magazines.

The country press, weeklies and some small dailies, except where they are controlled by "boiler plate," are still free. Country editors are the successors of Horace Greeley, James Gordon Bennett and Old Man Dana[7] and maybe, I say maybe, Hearst.

One of Truman's last unmailed communications concerns John Kennedy's assassination. Author William Manchester, in preparation for his book Death of a President, *planned to interview him in Independence and, upon advice from Rose Conway, sent ahead three questions he wanted to ask: Where did the former President first learn of Kennedy's death? At what moment did he judge Vice-President Lyndon Johnson officially became President? What could he recall about conversations with people during his attendance at Kennedy's funeral? "Questions have been answered by conditions as they developed. So just file it," HST wrote across Manchester's query. Then he changed his mind, agreed to meet with the author, and recorded some preliminary responses to the three questions.*

Eight days later, Manchester's eighty-year-old witness to history tripped and fell in his bathroom, hit his head, cracked his ribs, and never again regained his vitality. The interview was scrapped and the old man's recollections about a young man's death went into the files.

October 5, 1964

I first learned that President Kennedy had been shot while visiting in Kansas City at the Muehlebach Hotel. I did not

---

[7]   Nineteenth-century New York *Sun* editor Charles Anderson Dana.

know at that time that he had been killed. This I learned a short time later while I was in the car.

Lyndon Johnson became President officially immediately after he was sworn in on the airplane taking him to Washington.[8]

As I was preparing to fly to Washington, I received a call from President Johnson telling me that a plane was being sent for me and I was able to arrive the day before the funeral. I went directly to the Blair House. Shortly after arriving there we rode over to the White House to call on Mrs. Kennedy. I found her as I had expected, remarkably self possessed and poised, but to me the deep sadness in her eyes came through. She said to me her husband, the President, spoke of me often and with much feeling and understanding of what we tried to do, and I found myself choked up with emotion.

It is difficult for one who has lived through the Presidency in the many trials and burdens that go with it, not to realize the enormity of the tragedy that had befallen the nation and the tragic blow that was visited on his family, and particularly on the wife of the President.

---

[8] Truman was mistaken. By law, the Vice-President became President immediately upon the young Chief Executive's death.

Chapter 9

KINFOLK,
NEIGHBORS,
AND OTHERS

Desk Note
[1950s]
. . . In the 1890s and early 1900s young people had great times in the country districts of the middle west. There were unpolluted streams, ponds, small lakes and beautiful pastures adjoining small centers of population where boys could enjoy games, swimming, ball games, tag and long adventurous walks. Walks which might take them to small creeks and perhaps to great rivers.

Evenings were spent in the yards and blocks around the homes of the good people who were the parents of the neighborhood boys and girls.

Games, hide and seek, run-sheep-run, catch as catch can, wrestling matches were entertainment for the young people of the neighborhood.

Speech Note
November 28, 1956
. . . I've been from Aroostook the potato county in Maine to San Diego, California, from Seattle and Bellingham Wash-

ington to Key West, Florida, from Minnesota to Louisiana, and all the states in between east, west, north and south. While they are all great in some particular, Missouri is great in all particulars.

I've been to many countries in Europe, South and Central America. I've been to Mexico and Canada. And while I had great receptions and cordial welcomes in all of them — I still favor Missouri as the best place to live.

I've had every political office, nearly, from precinct to President of the United States, and I came back home to live at the end of it all. . . .

He always came home, this man from Independence. He could have parlayed his position as President into a six-figure yearly income and bought a Manhattan townhouse, a beachfront spread, or a Spanish-style mansion in Palm Springs. But Harry and Bess preferred that two-story clapboard house in Independence that Bess's grandfather had built in the neighborhood where they played as children. Across the street to the north lived his cousins, the Noland sisters; behind them with adjoining backyards were Bess's two brothers, the Wallaces. A block south stands the Presbyterian Church where in Sunday School Harry had met his lifelong sweetheart, "the most beautiful girl I ever saw." And a few blocks beyond is the courthouse square where Harry's political career had begun thirty years before.

In early April 1945, Ethel Noland had gotten a letter from Bess who wrote from Washington, "I hope the Boston Globe man is a mighty bad prognosticator." The newspaperman, thinking President Roosevelt looked awfully ill, had "just in case" sent someone out to Independence to gather background information on Harry. Bess reported she had recently talked with FDR and that he looked "fine" to her. "He's a little deaf," she conceded, "but that's not going to wreck him."

Twelve days later, however, Harry was summoned to the White House, and Bess was soon packing to live there. She hated "that Great White Jail," as she and her husband called it, and she spent a great deal of time in Independence. So a lonely President, unable to get away from Washington as much as she, wrote a good many letters home to Bess, to his sister Mary Jane, and to other family members.

Bess and Mary Jane burned Harry's letters: history or no history, they were nobody's business but theirs. A few survive, however, including the one found tucked away in a White House desk together with its unused envelope addressed in HST's hand to "Mrs. Harry S. Truman, 219 North Delaware St., Independence, Mo." Busy Harry, having had to cut short his first presidential trip home for Christmas, was clearly in the dog house.

Dec. 28, 1945

Dear Bess:

Well I'm here in the White House, the great white sepulcher of ambitions and reputations. I feel like a last year's bird's nest which is on it's second year. Not very often I admit I am not in shape. I think maybe that exasperates you too, as a lot of other things I do and pretend to do exasperate you. But it isn't intended for that purpose.

When you told me I might as well have stayed in Washington so far as you were concerned I gave up, cussed [*Senator*] Vandenberg, told the Secretary of Agriculture to give all the damned cotton away for all I cared and then smiled over the phone at Henry Wallace and I'm afraid hurt Adm. Leahy's feelings by not asking him to go on the boat. At least Matt said I did and I called the old admiral up and asked him to go. He was as pleased as David was with his telescope.

You can never appreciate what it means to come home as I did the other evening after doing at least 100 things I didn't want to do and have the only person in the world whose approval and good opinion I value, look at me like I'm something the cat dragged in and tell me I've come in at last because I couldn't find any reason to stay away. I wonder why we are made so that what we really think and feel we cover up?

This head of mine should have been bigger and better proportioned. There ought to have been more brain and a larger bump of ego or something to give me an idea that there can be a No. 1 man in the world. I didn't want to be. But, in spite of opinion to the contrary, Life & Time say I am.

If that is the case you, Margie and everyone else who may have any influence on my actions must give me help and assistance, because no one ever needed help and assistance as I do now. If I can get the use of the best brains in the country and a little bit of help from those I have on a pedestal at home the job will be done. If I can't, no harm will be done because the country will know that Shoop, the Post Dispatch, Hearst, Cissy and Patterson were right.

Kiss my baby and I love you in season & out.

Harry

Next to Independence, the Trumans (especially Harry) liked Key West, Florida, and it became their favorite cold-weather vacation retreat. In 1947, during HST's first stay in the "winter White House," a ten-room West Indian–style white frame house at the Navy's sub base there,[1] daughter Margaret ("Margie" to her folks) made her national singing debut over ABC radio. John Spottswood, owner of the local

---

[1] The Navy vacated the sub base in the early seventies. By 1981 Truman's winter White House looked like a relic from a film set used for an Alfred Hitchcock mystery movie, its grounds cluttered with trash and uprooted trees, its interior walls water-streaked by tropical storms that warped roof shingles and side shutters could not deny, its rooms devoid of furniture after vandals had carried off most of it.

*Mutual network station, arranged to pipe the ABC program
from Miami to his station and to Truman's quarters.*

*Margaret's proud dad returned to Washington to find congratulatory messages waiting. He started to answer each personally but abandoned the effort when the compliments kept
pouring in to the White House. Instead he sent out a short
formal acknowledgment to the writers. One of the sixteen
individualized letters he didn't mail follows:*

March 22, 1947

Dear Miss Allen;

You were more than kind to write me as you did concerning Margaret's radio debut last Sunday evening, and of
course, it is gratifying to know that you were so well pleased
with her renditions. The good wishes of Margaret's friends
means as much to me as to her.

Please accept my thanks for your letter.

Very sincerely yours,

*But, alas, some music critics judged Margaret's talent in
less complimentary terms. When she toured California that
summer, the President got word that not everyone appreciated Margie's singing. "Some 'mean critics' had panned her
performance," Truman wrote his sister, Miss Mary Jane in
Grandview, Missouri. "If ever I meet one of the women who
writes for the News in Los Angeles," Harry assured Mary,
"I'll certainly box her ears because she lied. She said Margie
was off pitch, and she has perfect pitch."*

Washington Post *music critic Paul Hume felt the sting of
Truman's pen. In early December 1950, Hume critiqued
Miss Truman's Washington, D.C., concert, telling his readers
that Margaret's voice was "flat" and that he was mystified
that people kept paying to hear her. The President had a fit.
He was in a terrible mood anyway, because his friend since
high school days, press secretary Charlie Ross, had collapsed
and died at his desk shortly before Margaret's concert the*

night before. Truman wrote Hume a spasm that raised eyebrows across the land when Hume went public with the letter. In it, Truman threatened Hume with bodily disfigurement, and while not calling him an S.O.B. as so many newspapers reported, did describe Hume as lower than a "guttersnipe," saying that he hoped Hume would "accept that statement as a worse insult than a reflection on your ancestry."[2]

"Margie is the 'apple of my eye,'" the President later explained privately. "I admit I am violently prejudiced in her favor." He didn't care what critics said about him, "But when one of 'em jumps on Margie unfairly — well, I jump too."

When Margaret traveled to Europe the following summer, she made plans to visit the Pope in Rome. The Archbishop of Philadelphia, D. Cardinal Dougherty, composed a letter of introduction for her, and sent a copy to the President. He assured Margaret's father that she would receive a gracious welcome from the pontiff.

The President responded warmly but not as warmly as in the unsent letter he first wrote the Cardinal.

May 29, 1951

Your Eminence:

How can I ever express to you the gratitude that filled my heart when I received your wonderful letter of May twenty-third. I am sure that as a result of your gracious and generous action, Margaret will have a memorable visit to Rome, the highlight of which will, of course, be her audience with His Holiness, the Pope. My child is very dear to me and anyone who adds to her happiness wins my lasting affection.

With great respect,
Gratefully and sincerely,

---

2   The Hume letter became a collector's item. Truman was sent a news clipping in 1966 announcing a recent sale of the letter; the anonymous correspondent penned at the bottom of the clipping, "And they elected you President! If you knew what the average American thinks of you, you would hang yourself!"

Margaret's European visit went so well that celebrated world adventurer Lowell Thomas suggested to the President that he consider sending Margaret to the Middle East, to Iran and several neighboring countries that were then, as now, undergoing turbulent change.

Thomas heard from the President, but the letter he received over Truman's signature was written in the stiff and formal prose of a presidential assistant. Truman filed away his own original reply to Thomas.

July 28, 1951

Dear Mr. Thomas:

I read your letter of July twentieth with a great deal of interest and I appreciate very much what you have to say about Margaret.

I have tried my best to prevent the White House from becoming entangled in Margaret's career. She wants to be a professional singer and she wants to be a singer on her merit and by her own efforts.

Her trip to Europe was purely a vacation for her and was not intended to be political in any way, but due to the fact that she is the daughter of the President, she had certain social obligations to meet. For the very reason that there was no motive behind her visit was the reason for its success.

I shall never use Margaret for any political purpose, and while I know your suggestion is from the heart, and that you believe a visit by her to Iran might be helpful, I of course, can't accept your suggestion. I believe Mr. Harriman will eventually work the matter out all right.

Sincerely yours,
Harry S. Truman

Meanwhile, music critic Hume was not forgotten.

In early February 1952, the President and Mrs. Truman attended a Washington piano recital by Gina Bachauer.

Next day Hume's newspaper review differed radically from Truman's recollection of the recital. He labored over Hume's Washington Post *column, underlining those things with which he disagreed. "Bunk!" he scribbled alongside Hume's declaration that Bachauer's rendition of the Liszt "Spanish Rhapsody" was "musically worthless." Where Hume criticized the pianist for using too much soft pedal on Haydn's E Minor Sonata, and too little pedal on Bach's Adagio, Truman retorted, "Bunk again!" and "How does he know? Bach is dead!"*

Dr. Glenn Dillard Gunn of the Washington Times-Herald also reviewed Bachauer's recital, calling it "the season's most impressive exhibition of pianistic art."

Truman wrote but did not mail a letter to Hume's boss, Washington Post *publisher Philip Graham, enclosing clippings of both men's reviews.*

Clippings from W. Post & Times Herald enclosed.

February 4, 1952

Dear Phil:

Why don't you fire this frustrated old fart and hire a music reviewer who knows what he's talking about? At least you should send somebody with him to a piano recital who knows the score.

This review is a disgraceful piece of poppycock. You should be ashamed of having printed it. You're not, of course, because the publicity sheets are never wrong.

Read Dr. Gunn's piece.

Sincerely,
H.S.T.

One of Harry Truman's sweet triumphs after he and Bess left public life and returned to Missouri was the honorary membership extended him by the exclusive Kansas City

*Club. Located near the Federal Reserve Bank Building in
downtown Kansas City, where Truman had his first post-
presidential office, he often went to the club for lunch.
Former political enemies, the city's richest (and very Republican) businessmen, now jockeyed beneath glittering chande-
liers to shake hands with the fella from the other side of the
tracks.*

*An undelivered handwritten note intended for club mem-
ber George Davis was found among the former President's
papers.*

[1950s]

Dear Mr. Davis:

I saw Joe Brown at lunch today with Ray Niles. They informed me that your pulse was up to 112. That sounds like
mine when I jump on a music critic of my daughter.

Ordinarily mine is only about 52. Let's compromise and
make it 72. Take care of yourself.

I hope you'll be all right shortly,

Sincerely,
Harry S. Truman

*One Kansas City honorary membership was declined,
however. Besieged by requests that he and Bess endorse a
wide range of civic causes in his retirement years, Truman
decided finally to draw the line. "No as politely as possible.
She's a nice lady," he instructed in a note attached to Mrs.
Russell Stover's letter asking him to bless her ballet group.
Not satisfied that the denial was sufficiently polite, HST directed, "File as it is."*

March 26, 1959

Dear Mrs. Stover:

Thank you very much for your letter of the twenty-second.
I am honored by your invitation to become an honorary

sponsor of The Kansas City Civic Ballet Association, but I do not feel that I should accept it.

Mrs. Truman and I have lent our names to so many civic projects in this community that we find ourselves forced to limit our associations to those we already have.

Otherwise, and I am sure that you will understand this position, the value of our support, whatever it may be, undoubtedly would be lessened.

Sincerely yours,

Harry S. Truman

Truman's early training as an artillery officer instilled in him a lifelong penchant for precision and orderliness. While President, he fretted when various municipalities and regions began setting their clocks ahead to practice an individualized form of daylight saving time. Afterward, as seen in this unmailed complaint, he fretted even more when he noticed that the clock atop the Pickwick Hotel across from his downtown Kansas City office didn't conform to any time.

December 17, 1956

Pickwick:

You have a clock over your bus depot that gives me a case of time-ophobia. I look at that clock every time I go to this Federal Reserve Building's privy, on floor 11.

When my watch and all four of my clocks say it is 9:25 A.M. Central Standard Time, that damned clock of yours will say it is 6:40. I don't know whether it is afternoon or forenoon or just half-way between Eastern Daylight Time and no time at all.

Just because you are named for Charles Dickens' Mr. Pickwick doesn't give you authority to mess up our local time.

It is bad enough when these municipalities like New York, Chicago, St. Louis and some others ball up the Standard

Time Zones. It took almost forty years to attain a sensible time zone setup for this round globe of ours and now we might just as well go back to meridian time of the 1820's. You shouldn't contribute to that confusion.

Harry S. Truman

In 1957, the former President moved his office to the recently completed Truman Library, situated conveniently near his home in Independence. Several years went by and Western Union decided to add another "convenience." The telegraph company, wanting to close down its Independence-based operations, installed a teletype receiver in Truman's Library office so that messages for him would rattle off a machine only a few steps away from his desk. Rather than appreciate the new setup, Truman hated it. He wanted the company to deliver his messages as before, and he said so in an undelivered protest.

November 25, 1960

Western Union:

Come and take this crazy receiver you have set up in my office.

It is a nuisance. When messages are sent to me they are supposed to be delivered and I'm not supposed to be your delivery agent. I'm telling all my friends to phone me.

The messages that come over this damned machine can't be read anyway.

Early risers in Independence became accustomed to seeing the former President on his morning walks, tipping his hat to the ladies, swinging his cane in cadence to 120 paces a minute. Sometimes he went up Delaware Street toward the library named after him. Other times he might be seen going down Lexington past the post office, heading toward the courthouse. That courthouse, thanks to him, was redesigned in 1933 to look a lot like Philadelphia's Independence Hall. And on top, a tower clock even today keeps good time and tolls each hour as it should.

By the fifties, however, Independence resembled only faintly that idyllic rural village adjoined by unpolluted streams and pastorial vistas depicted in Truman's nostalgic reminiscence about his youth. It had grown following World War II into a burgeoning bedroom community serving thousands of Kansas City's industrial workers. Consequently, among other urban improvements, Independence needed a new post office. Ironically, because its leading citizen had been President, it had to wait an extended time to get one. It would have looked too much like pork-barrel politics. Besides, a Republican followed Truman in the White House. That changed in 1961 when John Kennedy became President, and HST, now out of office eight years, pushed to obtain for Independence its long-awaited new postal facility along with a federal office building.

It was not an easy accomplishment, however. While the former President's local congressman, William Randall, was a Democrat, he was not Truman's kind of Democrat. Nor, with the way Washington ignored him on federal judgeships and other appointments, did Truman enjoy much influence with the new Kennedy Administration. In frustration, he turned to Missouri Senator Stuart Symington, whom he had promoted for the 1960 Democratic presidential nomination. The two men exchanged various letters on the subject, but HST withheld this one:

August 23, 1961

Dear Stuart:

I have your letter about the Post Office and Federal Office Building in Independence.

For your information, it has been my condition here in the 4th Congressional District to have two double barrelled shit asses as Congressmen.

My only recourse was to appeal to you as U. S. Senator. Mr. Long[3] had already used a precedent to inform the President that unless his man was made a Federal Judge there would not be a Federal Judge. Both Judges were recommended by the two Senators and so were the district attorneys for St. Louis and for Kansas City without consultation with the former President.

This old man has always considered himself as having had his turn in public affairs. It is nice however to have the successors appreciate his former service.

If you want to know the records and actions of the 4th District Congressmen, all you have to do is ask me!

> Sincerely,
> Harry S. Truman

"My Congressman has not done and won't do anything!" *the old man still complained to Congressman Richard Bolling (liberal Democrat who represented Kansas City) eight months after he had written an unmailed grievance to his 4th District Congressman, Bill Randall.*

                                                    March 9, 1962
Dear Bill:

I have just learned that you made a statement to the Post Office Committee of the House that you were not interested in the situation here in Independence insofar as it affect[s] you.

I am glad to know that and it was nice of you not to let me know of your appearance before the Committee.

> Sincerely yours,

---

3   Edward V. Long, Democratic senator from Missouri.

Kennedy's Postmaster General, J. Edward Day, also frus-trated Truman. Day wrote him about a new federal leasing policy, saying that the government would alleviate over-crowding at the Independence post office by renting a new postal facility to be constructed there by private investors on federally owned land. The Washington bureaucrat also ques-tioned the need for a federal office building in Independence, pointing out that a survey had yet to be taken on the matter.

The former chief executive's heated rejoinder went through two drafts: the second went into the U.S. Mail, the first into Rose Conway's file cabinet.

February 5, 1962

Dear Mr. Postmaster General:

Replying to yours of a few days ago (not dated) about the proposed cowshed addition to the Independence Post Office.

Back in the 1930s while I was United States Senator from Missouri, I obtained a lot at Osage and Lexington streets which contains 50,000 square feet. The objective was to ob-tain a post office and Federal Office Building for Independ-ence, at that time a city of about 17,000 people. The city now has 80,000 inhabitants. Independence needs a Post Office and Federal Office Building.

The United States Government has owned the corner at Osage and Lexington Streets across Lexington Street from the present post office for about twenty five years. We've never had a Congressman who was interested in the welfare of this Capitol of Jackson County, Missouri. Since I obtained this site for a real Federal Office Building and post office the 4th District has never had a man in Congress whose interest is his district. Look over the title to this lot which contains 50,000 square feet.

It was obtained for the Post Office Department and the title placed in the Government of the United States. That lot is worth about $2.50 or $3.00 a square foot — that is anywhere between $150,000 and $250,000 and you are proposing a Dixon-Yates on it. To give away Government property and then pay rent on it!

Why don't you go ahead and build your substitute on the government owned lot in such a way that it can be used in a real post office and an office building in the future? Why should the U.S. Gov't. give away property it already owns for the purpose we both have in mind — *and pay rent* on its own property?

I haven't exploded publicly on this — but if it is necessary I shall do it.

> Yours truly,
> Harry S. Truman

Truman did not have to explode publicly, however. "Talk[ed] to the PMG [Postmaster General] — 3/12/62. He wants to do the job," HST jotted triumphantly. On April 4, 1966, Independence's eighty-two-year-old political champ purchased the first stamps sold at the government-owned post office in the city's new federal building located at the corner of Osage and Lexington streets.

Some months earlier, about the time groundbreaking took place for the federal building, Truman was asked to advance another local effort. Russell V. Dye wrote from Liberty, a town across the Missouri River from Independence, that after sixteen years as chairman of his draft board, he had come up with a number of recommendations to improve selective service. Dye detailed them for the former Commander-in-Chief, and apologized at the end for his messy typing, explaining, "Fell off the roof Monday while shingling."

Dye's misfortune elicited a story that Truman decided he best not mail. "I am not in a position to relate the story here," he wrote Dye, "but will tell it to you when you stop in."

September 18, 1964

Dear Mr. Dye:

Thanks for your letter of advice. Draft Boards do not appreciate such communications from "has beens" — so I did not advise them.

I notice at the end of your letter, you fell off the roof while nailing on some shingles. It brought up a story of the great Mon Wallgren about a Swede who had the same experience.

This Swede was in Alaska as a prospector, used up his supplies and started for Dawson City. A blizzard caught him and he stopped at the first house. Only the woman of the place was at home. He asked if he could stay the night. She gave him permission to stay.

He had a lot of blankets with him and when she came down and told him she was cold, he gave her another blanket.

Went on to Dawson the next day, and then to the United States and began following his trade as carpenter. He was nailing shingles on a roof — fell off and broke his leg.

When asked how it happened, he said he "ves tinkin" about what "dot voman wanted" in Alaska. It occurred to him and he said, "I tried to kick myself in the behind, fell off de roof and broke the leg."

A month later, entering his bathroom, the old patriot tripped and fell himself. His cracked ribs and head wound healed, but, plagued by a circulatory ailment that affected his balance, Truman's health gradually deteriorated. Leaning heavily on his cane outside his office door one Friday in the summer of 1966, he waved a shaky goodbye and, as he had so many times before, told Truman Library security officer Bill Story, "I'll see you Monday morning, Sergeant." "But he never came back; he never made it back," Story explains. "He'd drive by once in a while and look at the Library

from the outside."[4] *Forced finally to retire from public involvement, to give up his regular morning walks, Truman
spent his last six years confined largely within the walls of
the old house Bess's grandfather had built. "Reading is our
best diversion these days," the old man explained to his niece,
Martha Ann Swoyer, in a letter he wrote about a year before
he died.*

*But, of course, that's not the way folks in Independence
remember Harry Truman. Following his death they erected
a statue of him in the courthouse square. Cane in hand, it is
a bronzed figure of Harry frozen in half stride as though he
were walking out of the county courthouse. True to form,
the sculptor put the cane in the left hand, for in real life the
right hand was busy tipping a hat to the ladies or shaking
hands with a passerby. It's a pretty fair likeness. It's almost
as if Harry were on his way to the train depot after jotting
Bess this note that two decades earlier had somehow ended
up in his desk drawer.*

Oct. 2, 60

Bess:
I have decided to walk to
the station. It will be my
morning walk both ways.
The grip isn't heavy.
Harry S. Truman[5]

---

[4] The President did return twice to the Library, but for only brief visits,
once in 1969 when President Richard M. Nixon presented him a piano
Truman had played in the White House, and again one evening to view
a short film at Christmastime a year before he died.

[5] Seemingly out of place, his formal signature was signed out of habit.

SOURCE NOTES

Abbreviations

Memoirs I	*Year of Decisions,* Harry S. Truman (Garden City, N.Y.: Doubleday, 1955)
Memoirs II	*Years of Trial and Hope,* Harry S. Truman (Garden City, N.Y.: Doubleday, 1956)
OTR	*Off the Record,* edited by Robert H. Ferrell (New York: Harper, 1980)
Public Papers	*Public Papers of the Presidents: Harry S. Truman* (Washington: Government Printing Office, 1961–66)
PPF	Post-Presidential Files
PSF	President's Secretary's File

Unless otherwise indicated, references are to documents contained in the Papers of Harry S. Truman.

Chapter 1
HARRY TRUMAN, LETTER WRITER

"You're not going to send this," Oral history interview with Matthew J. Connelly by Jerry N. Hess, November 30, 1967, Harry S. Truman Library, 1969, pp. 1979–80.

"A letter or a memo considered by the President . . ." Speech for Westminster College, Fulton, Mo., April 13, 1954: PPF, Speech File, "Speech Drafts, 1954," Box 7.

"You know, I'm no scholar in any line . . ." Truman to Dean Acheson, July 16, 1957: PPF, Name File, "Acheson, Dean," Box 1.

Chapter 2
THE PRESS

"The Columnists & the Publisher" [1950s] (handwritten): PPF, Desk File, "Personal Notes—HST," Set II, Box 3.

"If [Pulitzer] and his ilk . . ." Truman to Nellie Noland, November 3, 1951: "HST to the Noland Family," Box 2, Papers of Mary Ethel Noland.

"My Dear Mr. Cooper" [Early June 1974] (partially handwritten): PSF, "C" folder 3, Box 114.

"Gentlemen," July 9, 1947 (handwritten): PSF, "Virginia, Charlottesville," Box 105. Also in *OTR*, pp. 114–15.

"Your reply to my comment . . ." May [sic] 15, 1949 (handwritten): On reverse side of Julius Ochs Adler to Truman, June 15, 1949, PSF, "A" Box 305.

"My dear Mr. Roper," December 30, 1948 (handwritten): PSF, "Personal Memos, 1948," Box 333.

"Dear Mr. Roper," September 22, 1951: PSF, "Ri" Box 293.

"Dear Mr. Southern," July 8, 1949 (handwritten): PSF, "Personal Memos, 1949," Box 333. Also in *OTR*, pp. 159–60.

Garrett L. Smalley to Truman, October 12, 1949: PSF, "S1" Box 294.

"Dear Garrett," October 18, 1949: Ibid.

Burt Drummond to Truman, May 20, 1954: PPF, Name File, "Do" Box 24.

"Dear Mr. Drummond," May 26, 1954: Ibid.

"Dear Mr. Graham," June 5, 1950: PSF, "Gr" Box 286.

"Dear Mr. Cater," August 12, 1950: PSF, "C" folder 1, Box 114.

"My dear Mr. Kent," September 2, 1951 (handwritten): PSF, "Personal Memos, 1951," Box 333.

"Dear Mr. Greene," October 2, 1954: PPF, Name File, "Ka" Box 45.

"If I could have gotten my hands on him . . ." Truman to Mary Jane Truman, February 11, 1948: PPF, Memoirs, Box 47.

[Dear Mr. Holmes], [Late January 1956]: PPF, Name File, "Wi" Box 92.

"Memo to Wayne W. Parrish" [Mid-July 1951] (handwritten): PSF, "Notes—undated," Box 334.

"My dear Arthur," October 7, 1951 (handwritten): PSF, "Personal Memos, 1951," Box 333. First published without Krock's name in William Hillman, *Mr. President* (New York: Farrar, Straus & Young, 1952), p. 47. Also in *OTR*, pp. 218–19.

Tony Vaccaro to Truman, April 9, 1950: PSF, "Vaccaro, Tony," Box 327.
"Memorandum for: Tony Vaccaro," April 12, 1950: Ibid.
"Dear New Yorker," January 8, 1952 (handwritten): PSF, "Personal Memos, 1952," Box 333. Also in *OTR*, pp. 227–28.

Chapter 3
THE WAR, THE A-BOMB, & AFTER

"Call in [CIO's] Phil Murray . . ." [ca. June 1946] (handwritten): PSF, "Personal Memos, 1946," Box 333.
"I wrote you a longhand letter . . ." Truman to Dean Acheson, April 12, 1957: PPF, Name File, "Acheson, Dean, 1956–57," Box 1.
"Dear Dean," March 15, 1957 (handwritten): Ibid. Also in *OTR*, pp. 348–49.
Herbert Feis to Truman, April 16, 1962: PPF, Secretary's Office File, "Letters, special," Box 19.
"My dear Mr. Feis" [Late April 1962] (handwritten): Ibid.
"We'll send it air mail . . ." attached to Truman to Chairman of the Hiroshima City Council, March 12, 1958: PPF, Secretary's Office File, Box 12.
"Dear Kup," August 5, 1963: PPF, Name File, "Chicago *Sun Times,*" Box 15.
U.S. commanders committed a "master mistake," Lewis H. Brown, *A Report on Germany* (New York: Farrar, Straus, 1947), p. 7.
"My dear Mr. Brown" [August 30, 1947]: PSF, "Br–Bz" Box 113.
"My dear Jim," January 5, 1946 (handwritten): PSF, "Personal Memos, 1946," Box 333. Appears in *Memoirs I*, pp. 551–52 and in *OTR*, pp. 79–80.
Grant W. Oakes (United Farm Equipment and Metal Workers of America) to Truman (wire), September 10, 1946: PSF, "O" Box 132.
"Dear Mr. Oakes," September 12, 1946: Ibid. Also in *OTR*, p. 92.
"Your Majesties," January 3, 1963: PPF, Name File, "Greece," Box 34.
"Dear Joe," November 24, 1945: PSF, "Ba–Bh" Box 113.
"Dear Mr. Harlamert," January 3, 1952: PSF, "H" Box 312.
George H. Fallon to Truman, November 7, 1951: PSF, "F" Box 311.
"Dear Congressman Fallon," November 13, 1951: Ibid.
"My dear Henry," November 18, 1952 (handwritten): PSF, "Personal Memos, 1952," Box 333.
Henry F. Grady to Truman, November 22, 1952: PSF, "G" Box 311.
"Dear Henry," November 27, 1952 (handwritten): Ibid.

Chapter 4
STOPPING REDS IN ASIA

"Frank Pace called . . ." June 30, 1950 (handwritten): PSF, "MacArthur, Douglas—Messages, President Truman," Box 129. First published in Margaret Truman, *Harry S. Truman* (New York: Morrow, 1973), p. 469. Also in *OTR*, p. 185.

"I'm so tired . . ." Quoted in Robert and LaPrelle Weatherford interview with editor, Phoenix, Az., November 5, 1978.

Robert Hale to Truman, June 21, 1950: PSF, "Ha–He" Box 121.

"Dear Congressman Hale," June 28, 1950: Ibid.

Hazel M. Earnest to Truman, January 4, 1951: PSF, "E" Box 118.

"My dear Mrs. Earnest," February 8, 1951: Ibid.

"sucked into a bottomless pit," quoted in *Memoirs II*, p. 388.

"My son died for no reason . . ." Earnest to Truman, January 4, 1951: PSF, "E" Box 118.

Harold E. Stassen to Truman, April 28, 1951: PSF, "Sn–Sz" Box 135.

"Dear Governor," April 30, 1951: Ibid.

"Dear John," November 28, 1952 (handwritten): PSF, "Personal Memos, 1952," folder 1, Box 333.

"To: Philip L. Graham," December 4, 1952 (handwritten): Ibid.

"My dear Chief Choi," November 4, 1952: PPF, Name File, "Korea— Choi Chi Whan," Box 46.

"Truman was the one President . . ." Arthur Krock, *Memoirs* (New York: Funk & Wagnalls, 1968), p. 221.

"Dear Arthur," September 11, 1952 (handwritten): PSF, "K" Box 314. Also in *OTR*, pp. 270–71.

Press statements on Vietnam, "side-line hecklers," "short memories," and "turning their backs on us," February 16, 1965: PPF, Secretary's Office File, "Lyndon B. Johnson," Box 15; "full support" [for] "stand against aggression," March 19, 1967: PPF, Secretary's Office File, "Charles Murphy," Box 21.

"did not wish to make a statement at this time," attached to Charles Murphy to Truman, August 2, 1965: Ibid.

"Let us start to bring our men home . . ." Clark M. Clifford, "A Vietnam Reappraisal," *Foreign Affairs*, July 1969. Quoted in Clifford to Truman, June 18, 1969: PPF, Name File, "Clark Clifford," Box 18.

"Dear Clark" [Late June 1969]: Ibid.

Chapter 5
RUNNING THE GOVERNMENT

Diary Entries, March 24–November 1, 1949 (handwritten): PSF, "Diary 1949," Box 278.

Raymond B. Kimbrell to Truman, March 22, 1949: President's Personal File, 200-A, "K" Box 437.

"My dear Mr. *Kimbrell*," April 12, 1949 (handwritten): PSF, "K" Box 314.

Eleanor Roosevelt to Truman, May 13, 1948: PSF, "Roosevelt, Eleanor," Box 321.

"Dear Mrs. Roosevelt," May 17, 1948: Ibid. A shorter draft dated May 22 is in *OTR,* pp. 137–38.

"Dear Jim," [June 1946]: PSF, "M" Box 316.

"Dear Mr. Pusey," May 6, 1950: PSF, "P" Box 132.

"Dear Clint," September 24, 1949: PSF, "Anderson, Clinton P.," Box 281.

"I am taking that report for what it means . . ." and "The only comment I can make . . ." Press Conference, May 18, 1950: *Public Papers* (1950), p. 419.

"Dear John," May 22, 1950: PSF, "Mc—general" Box 128.

"I do not care to comment . . ." Press Conference, March 20, 1952: *Public Papers* (1952–53), p. 206.

"Dear Franklin," [February 15, 1952]: PSF, "Ri" Box 293.

"Dear Burt," April 28, 1952: PSF, "Wheeler, Burton K.," Box 328.

"Dear Francis," January 16, 1952: PSF, "Bi–Bl" Box 113.

"Dear Jonathan," February 26, 1950 (handwritten): PSF, "Daniels, Jonathan," Box 309. Also in *OTR,* p. 174.

"Dear Brother Dewey," June 13, 1949: PSF, "D" Box 117.

"Dear Senator," April 4, 1946: PSF, "W" Box 327.

"My dear Millard," March 4, 1949 (handwritten): PSF, "T" Box 324.

"Dear Adolph," May 25, 1949: PSF, "Sa–Sm" Box 135.

William O. Douglas to Truman, July 1, 1952: PSF, "Douglas, William O.," Box 118.

"Dear Bill," July 9, 1952: Ibid.

"Memorandum for: Mrs. Ruth B. Shipley," September 17, 1952: PSF, "Acheson, Dean," Box 281.

"To the Treasurer of the United States," December 26, 1961 (handwritten): PPF, Secretary's Office File, "T" Box 32. Also in *OTR,* pp. 398–99.

Chapter 6
HUMAN GREED AND HUMAN NEED

Diary Entries, 1930–31 (handwritten): PSF, "Longhand Notes, Harry S. Truman, County Judge," Box 334.

Diary Entries, March 26, 1949, September 2, 1949 (handwritten): PSF, "Diary 1949," Box 278.

Arkansas Speech, July 2, 1952: *Public Papers* (1952–53), p. 460.

State of the Union Message, January 21, 1946: *Public Papers* (1946), pp. 38, 50–51.

C. Donald Dallas to Truman, January 22, 1946: PSF, "Wage-Price Data," Box 141.

"My dear Mr. Dallas" [Late January 1946]: Ibid.

"Dear Senator McKellar," March 2, 1946: PSF, "Mc—general" Box 128.

"Dear Jim," December 7, 1946: PSF, "Patton, James G.," Box 292.

"My dear Mr. Marcus," July 12, 1949: PSF, "M" Box 316. Also in *OTR,* pp. 160–61.

"This is just the same old fight," Press Conference, May 10, 1951: *Public Papers* (1951), p. 276.

"Dear Congressman Cooley," June 15, 1951: PSF, "C" folder 4, Box 114.

John Gates to Truman, February 2, 1948 (wire): PSF, "G" Box 311.

"My dear Mr. Gates," February 5, 1948: Ibid.

"I have had some bitter disappointments . . ." *Memoirs II,* p. 23.

Ben Turoff to Truman, April 1, 1949: PSF, "Tr" Box 295.

"My dear Ben" [April 12, 1949]: Ibid.

"The selfish interests have always . . ." Labor Day Address, September 5, 1949: *Public Papers* (1949), pp. 461–63.

"Dear [John]" [Mid August 1949]: PSF, "L" Box 125.

"Dear Mrs. Heinrich," December 5, 1962: PPF, Name File, "He" Box 38.

"Dear Mr. Ronald," August 29, 1951: PSF, "Ri" Box 293.

"Dear John" [Early October 1949]: PSF, "R" Box 321.

Charles W. Tobey to Truman, March 26, 1951: PSF, "T" Box 324.

"Dear Senator Tobey," March 27, 1951: Ibid.

"I got a letter from a fellow . . ." Address at Americans for Democratic Action banquet, May 17, 1952: *Public Papers* (1952–53), p. 345.

"Dear Amon," April 25, 1952: PSF, "Carter, Amon," Box 307. A shorter but similarly worded unmailed letter was written to another Texan, Galloway Calhoun, April 28, 1952: PSF, "C" Box 306.

"I see no good reason . . ." Veto of Bill concerning Title to Offshore Lands, May 29, 1952: *Public Papers:* (1952–53), p. 381.

Amon Carter to Truman, June 16, 1952: PSF, "Carter, Amon," Box 307.

"Dear Mr. Carter," June 21, 1952: Ibid.

Chapter 7
DEMOCRATS OR HIGH HATS?

Diary Entry, October 29, 1949 (handwritten): PSF, "Diary, 1949," Box 278.

Desk Note, August 12, 1952 (handwritten): PSF, "Personal Memos, 1952," Box 333.

Desk Note, December 28, 1962 (handwritten): PPF, Desk File, "Personal Notes," Box 3. Also in *OTR,* pp. 406–07.

"You know, I have known people . . ." Remarks at Granite City, Illinois, November 1, 1952: *Public Papers* (1952–53), p. 1037.

"My dear Jim," May 17, 1946 (handwritten): PSF, "Pendergast, James," Box 320.

"Dear Jim" [Late March 1951]: PSF, "Pendergast, James," Box 292.

"My dear Mr. Kent," March 5, 1950 (handwritten): PSF, "Personal Memos, 1950," Box 333. Also in *OTR*, pp. 174–75.

"I am in the midst of the most terrible struggle . . ." Truman to Ralph E. Truman, March 26, 1950: "Corres., 1950," Box 1, Papers of Ralph E. Truman.

"My dear Senator," [February 11, 1950]: PSF, "McCarthy, Joseph," Box 128. Also in *OTR*, p. 172.

"Dear Mr. Tugwell" [December 12, 1950]: PSF, "Tugwell, Rexford G.," Box 295.

Richard Bergstrom (Webster Quimmly Society) to Truman, September 25, 1961 (wire): PPF, Name File, "Ba" Box 5.

"Why don't you believe it?" [Late September 1961]: Ibid.

"Dear Alben," May 27, 1950: PSF, "Barkley, Mr. & Mrs. Alben W.," Box 306.

"Dear Paul," June 28, 1980: PSF, "Fitzpatrick, Paul E.," Box 285.

"Dear Stu," May 12, 1952: PSF, "Symington, W. Stuart," Box 324.

"Dear Bob," August 15, 1952: PSF, "T" Box 324.

"My dear Governor" [Mid August 1952] (handwritten): PSF, "Longhand notes, undated," Box 334. Also in *OTR*, pp. 268–69.

"If he wants to see me . . ." Press Conference, September 18, 1952: *Public Papers* (1952–53), p. 583.

"My dear Senator Sparkman" [Late August 1952] (handwritten): PSF, "Personal Memos, 1952," Box 333.

"Dear Governor" [Late August 1952] (handwritten): PSF, "Longhand Notes, undated," Box 334. Also in *OTR*, pp. 266–67.

"Dear Mr. Fitzpatrick" [Late February 1956]: PPF, Name File, "Nixon, Richard," Box 66.

W. L. Harriman to Truman, November 24, 1958 (wire): PPF, Desk File, "Corres., general, 1918–64," Box 1. Also in *OTR*, p. 375.

"L. A. [sic] Harriman . . ." [Late November 1958] (handwritten): Ibid.

"Dear Mr. Graham," December 15, 1952: PSF, "Gr–Gz" Box 121.

"Dear Doctor Burnette," November 17, 1952: PSF, "Br" Box 282.

"Mr. Cow Fever [is] ignorant of history . . ." December 25, 1952 (handwritten): PSF, "Personal Memos, 1952," Box 333.

"Dear Jiggs," July 23, 1956: PPF, Name File, "Donohue, F. Joseph," Box 24.

William P. Gauss to Truman, September 2, 1956: PPF, Trip File, "Ottumwa, Iowa, Sept. 1," Box 10.

"Dear Mr. Gauss," September 6, 1956: Ibid.

"Dear Jack," September 18, 1956: PPF, Name File, "*Look* Magazine data," Box 53.

"My dear Ike," November 28, 1956 (handwritten): PPF, Secretary's Office File, "Eisenhower, Dwight D.," Box 7. Also in *OTR*, p. 341.

"My only objective . . ." August 13, 1957: PPF, Name File, "Murphy, Charles," Box 62.

"Dear Sam," July 8, 1959 (handwritten): PPF, Desk File, "Corres., general, 1918–64," Box 1.

"Senator, are you certain . . ." New York *Times*, July 3, 1960.

"Dear Joe," January 31, 1960 (handwritten): PPF, Desk File, "Corres., general, 1918–64," Box 1.

"Dear Dean," August 26, 1960 (handwritten): PPF, Desk File, "Corres., Dean Acheson, 1956–62," Box 1. Also in *OTR*, pp. 390–91.

"He [Nixon] is a dangerous man . . ." Truman to Acheson, October 9, 1960: PPF, Name File, "Acheson, Dean," Box 1.

"Dear Mr. Peacock," September 5, 1963: PPF, Secretary's Office File, "Letters Held," Box 19.

"Dear Crosby," September 5, 1962 (handwritten): PPF, Secretary's Office File, "K" Box 16. Also in *OTR*, pp. 404–05.

Chapter 8
HARRY TRUMAN, HISTORIAN

Diary Entry, May 14, 1934 (handwritten): PSF, "Longhand Notes, Harry S. Truman, County Judge," Box 334.

Desk Note, ca. 1954 (handwritten): PPF, Desk File, "Personal Notes—HST," Box 3. Also in Robert H. Ferrell, ed., *The Autobiography of Harry S. Truman* (Boulder, Colo.: Colorado Associated University Press, 1980), p. 115.

"Dear Roy," June 12, 1950 (handwritten): PSF, "Roberts, Roy A.," Box 321. A shorter second draft, same date, appears in *OTR*, pp. 180–82.

"Your Kansas City history . . ." Truman to Roy Roberts, June 17, 1950: PSF, "Roberts, Roy A.," Box 321.

Roy A. Roberts to Truman, June 26, 1950: Ibid.

"Dear Mr. Littell" [Mid September 1950] (partially handwritten): PSF, "Li" Box 289.

"Dear Mr. Lieberson" [Late January 1955] (partially handwritten): PPF, Secretary's Office File, "CBS" Box 5.

Seward F. Sanford to Truman, December 12, 1954: PPF, Name File, "Sa" Box 75.

"Dear Mr. Sanford" [Mid December 1954]: Ibid.

Hugh C. Ellis to Truman, November 30, 1954: PPF, Name File, "E" Box 25.

"Dear Mr. Ellis," December 6, 1954: Ibid.

"You know, if it weren't for . . ." Truman to Samuel I. Rosenman, July
21, 1955: PPF, Secretary's Office File, "Rosenman, Samuel," Box 27.
"What I am trying to do . . ." Truman to Dean Acheson, June 7, 1955:
PPF, Name File, "Acheson, Dean," Box 1.
"Dear Roy," March 24, 1956: PPF, Name File, "Roy & Mrs. Roy A.
Roberts," Box 74.
"Dear Bill," October 31, 1959 (handwritten): PPF, Desk File, "Corres.,
general, 1918–64," Box 1.
"Bob, I've got to make a decision . . ." Quoted in Robert and LaPrelle
Weatherford interview with editor, Phoenix, Az., November 5, 1978.
"This fifty cents to her . . ." Truman to David D. Lloyd, December 10,
1953: "Truman, Harry S.," Box 12, Papers of David D. Lloyd.
"Dear Abe" [September 1954]: PPF, Name File, "Charles S. Murphy,
1953–54," Box 62.
"My dear Mr. Whiteway," January 21, 1959 (handwritten): PPF, Desk
File, "Corres., general, 1918–64," Box 1. Also in *OTR*, pp. 378–79.
"Dear Dr. Brooks," February 25, 1963: PPF, Name File, "Iturbi Concert
—March 30, 1963," Box 42.
"Let's go out and visit the customers . . ." Quoted in Milton F. Perry
interview with editor, Kansas City, Mo., September 22, 1980.
Mrs. Robert T. Foley to Truman, November 27, 1961: PPF, Name File,
"White House Data," Box 91.
"Dear Mrs. Foley" [Early December 1961] (partially handwritten): Ibid.
"Mr. Bernstein," January 7, 1955 (handwritten): PPF, Name File, "B"
Box 5.
Thomas Hart Benton to Truman, January 9, 1964: PPF, Name File,
"Presidents' Pictures," Box 71.
"Dear Tom," January 17, 1964: Ibid.
"They call it 'the Truman Library' . . ." Truman to Tom C. Clark, October
13, 1962: PPF, Name File, "Clark, Tom," Box 18.
"You know when monuments . . ." Truman to Jeff Lockhart, August 27,
1962: PPF, Secretary's Office File, "President's rating," Box 24.
"Dear Mr. Grande," November 21, 1961: PPF, Name File, "*Look* Mag-
azine Data," Box 52.
"When you get groups of kids . . ." Quoted in Milton F. Perry interview
with editor, Kansas City, Mo., September 22, 1980.
William I. Nichols to Truman, July 11, 1963: PPF, Name File, "*This
Week* Magazine," Box 84.
"Dear Mr. Nichols," July 18, 1963 (partially handwritten): Ibid.
"Dear Mr. Jones," July 29, 1955: PPF, Secretary's Office File, "CBS,"
folder 2, Box 5.
Merle Miller to Truman, April 15, 1963: PPF, Secretary's Office File,
"Miller, Merle," Box 21.
"Dear Mr. Miller," April 25, 1963: Ibid.
"Old man Sarnoff is not very fond of me . . ." Truman to Robert E.

Kintner, November 28, 1962: PPF, Secretary's Office File, "NBC," Box 22.

"Dear Mr. Nelson," January 22, 1964: Ibid.

"Dear Doctor Schlesinger" [Mid September 1960]: PPF, Name File, "Schlesinger, Arthur, Jr.," Box 78.

William Manchester to Truman, September 8, 1964: PPF, Name File, "Ma" Box 56.

"I first learned that President Kennedy had been shot . . ." October 5, 1964: Ibid.

Chapter 9
KINFOLK, NEIGHBORS, AND OTHERS

Desk Note [1950s] (handwritten): PPF, Desk File, "Personal Notes—HST," Set II, Box 3.

Speech Note, November 28, 1956 (handwritten): PPF, Speech File, "Speech Drafts, Apr.–Dec., 1956," Box 8.

"The most beautiful girl I ever saw . . ." Diary Note, May 1931 (handwritten): PSF, "Longhand Notes—County Judge," Box 334.

"I hope the Boston Globe man . . ." Bess Truman to Ethel Noland, March 30, 1945: "Bess Truman to Noland Family," Box 1, Papers of Mary Ethel Noland.

"Dear Bess," December 28, 1945 (handwritten): PSF, "Desk File," folder 2, Box 309. Also in *OTR*, pp. 75–76.

"Dear Miss Allen," March 22, 1947: PSF, "Truman, Margaret—debut (concert)," Box 326. Fifteen additional unmailed acknowledgments are also in this file.

"Some 'mean critics' had panned her performance . . ." Truman to Mary Jane Truman, August 26, 1947: PPF, Memoirs, Box 47.

"Margie is the 'apple of my eye' . . ." Truman to Joseph H. McConnell, December 10, 1950: PSF, "Mc–" Box 316.

"Your Eminence," May 29, 1951: PSF, "Truman, Margaret—European Trip, 1951," Box 326.

"Dear Mr. Thomas," July 28, 1951: PSF, "T" Box 138.

"Bunk!" newsclipping notations, no date (handwritten): PSF, "Music," Box 319.

"Dear Phil," February 4, 1952 (handwritten): PSF, "Personal Memos, 1952," folder 2, Box 333. The President altered his first draft, changing "fart" to read "fuddy duddy" and "fire" to "retire." This revised second draft, same date and also handwritten, was filed in PSF, "Music," Box 319.

"Dear Mr. Davis," [1950s] (handwritten): PPF, Secretary's Office File, "D" Box 6.

"Dear Mrs. Stover," March 26, 1959: PPF, Name File, "John M. Spottswood," Box 79.

"Pickwick," December 17, 1956 (handwritten): PPF, Desk File, "Personal Notes—HST," Box 3. Also in *OTR*, p. 345.

"Western Union," November 25, 1960 (handwritten): PPF, Secretary's Office File, "W" Box 34. Also in *OTR*, p. 392.

"Dear Stuart," August 23, 1961 (handwritten): PPF, Secretary's Office File, "Symington, Stuart—gen. corres.," folder 1, Box 32.

"My Congressman has not done . . ." Truman to Richard Bolling, November 20, 1962: PPF, Secretary's Office File, "Post Office—Independence," Box 24.

"Dear Bill," March 9, 1962: Ibid.

"Dear Mr. Postmaster General," February 5, 1962 (handwritten): Ibid. A shorter mailed version, same date, is in *OTR*, pp. 399–400.

"Talked to the PMG—3/12/62 . . ." (handwritten): jotted on J. Edward Day to Truman, February 8, 1962: Ibid.

Russell V. Dye to Truman, September 9, 1964: PPF, General File, "Dv–Dye" Box 84.

"I am not in a position . . ." Truman to Dye, September 23, 1964: Ibid.

"Dear Mr. Dye," September 18, 1964 (handwritten): PPF, Desk File, "Corres., general, 1918–64," Box 1.

"I'll see you . . ." William A. Story interview with editor, Seal Beach, Ca., July 14, 1979.

"Reading is our best . . ." Truman to Martha Ann Swoyer, November 4, 1971: PPF, Family Correspondence File, "Martha Ann Swoyer," Box 2.

"Bess," Oct. 2, 1960 (handwritten): PPF, Desk File, "Corres., family, 1958–1960," Box 1.

Oct. 2, 60

Bess:—

I have decided to walk to the ~~station~~. It will be my morning walk both ways.

The grip isn't heavy.

Harry Truman

INDEX

ABC radio, 173
Acheson, Alice, 33
Acheson, Dean, 8, 32, 37, 44, 47, 56, 71, 72, 150; and firing of MacArthur, 54–55; HST's assessment of, 15–16; unmailed HST letters to, 32–33, 46, 134–135
Acoff, Colonel, 49
Adams, Abigail, 159
Adams, John, 159
Adams, John Quincy, 23
Adler, Julius Ochs, unmailed HST letter to, 14
Alexander the Great, 27
Allen, Claudia E., unmailed HST letter to, 174
Allen, George, 79
American Aviation (magazine), 26
American China Policy Association, 83
American Medical Association, 96–97
Americans for Democratic Action (ADA), 74–75
Anderson, Clinton P., unmailed HST letter to, 69–70
Associated Press, 11, 28

Atlantic Pact, 15
atomic bomb, 4, 26, 32, 34–36

Bachauer, Gina, 176–177
Ball, Joseph H., unmailed HST letter to, 43
Barkley, Alben, 123, 253; unmailed HST letter to, 116–117
Barr, Robert W., 85
Bash, Thomas B., 85
Beard, Charles and Mary, 167
Bennett, James Gordon, 64, 168
Benny, Jack, 157
Benton, Thomas Hart, 159–160; unmailed HST letter to, 160–161
Berlin, Germany, 50, 57, 153
Bernhardt, Sarah, 143
Bernstein, Abraham, unmailed HST letter to, 159–160
Biddle, Francis, 74, 77; unmailed HST letter to, 75–76
Black, Hugo, 68
Black Sea Straits, 27, 33, 40
Blair House (Washington, D.C.), 123, 169
Block, Herb, 119
Bolling, Richard, 182
Bonaparte, Napoleon, 146

Boston *Globe,* 171
Bowen, Catherine Drinker, 161
Bowles, Chester, 77
Brewster, Owen, 122
Brian, Donald, 144
Bridges, Styles, 122
Brooks, Philip C., unmailed HST
    letter to, 157–158
Brown, Joe, 178
Brown, John, 135
Brown, Lewis H., 36; unmailed
    HST letter to, 37
Buchanan, James, 167
Bulgaria, 39, 40
Butler, Paul, 132
Byam, Less, 17
Byrd, Harry F., 62, 120, 131, 147
Byrnes, James F., 33, 38, 41, 42,
    152–153; unmailed HST letter
    to, 38–41
Burnette, Wells D., unmailed HST
    letter to, 128

Cain, Harry P., 80
Call-Bulletin. See San Francisco
    Call-Bulletin
Carol, Mildred, 7
Carter, Amon G., 104, 106;
    unmailed HST letters to, 105,
    106
Cashmore, John, 116–117, 118
Cater, Douglas, unmailed HST
    letter to, 23–24
Cawthorne, Joseph, 144
CBS television network, 163, 166
Central Intelligence Agency
    (CIA), 47
Chandler, A. B. ("Happy"), 152
Charles the Great, of France,
    145n2
Chiang Kai-shek, 19, 22, 50, 51, 58
Chicago *Daily News,* 21
Chicago *Sun Times,* 35
Chicago *Tribune,* 14, 125
China, 33, 40, 50–51; and Korean
    war, 50–51, 53, 56; *see also*
    Formosa
Choi (South Korean national
    police chief), unmailed HST
    letter to, 57

Churchill, Winston, 29, 32, 33, 34,
    36, 37, 61
Cincinnatus, Lucius Quinctius, 138
Civil War, American, 135, 146–
    147, 152
Clapp, Gordon, 62
Clark, Joseph, unmailed HST letter
    to, 133–134
Clark, Mark W., 44
Clay, Henry, 135
Clay, Lucius D., 36
Clemens, Cyril, 29
Clemens, Samuel (Mark Twain),
    29–30
Cleveland, Grover, 23, 113, 133,
    136
Cleveland *Plain Dealer,* 22
Clifford, Clark, 59; unmailed HST
    letter to, 60
Cockrell, Ewing, 30
Cockrell, Francis Marion, 30
Cohan, George M., et al., 143
communism: Red Scare, 19–20,
    26–27, 114–116; Voice of
    America as weapon against,
    11–12; *see also* Korean war;
    U.S.S.R.
Congress of Industrial Organiza-
    tion (CIO), 31, 41, 110
Connelly, Matthew J., 187
Conway, Rose, 6–8, 35, 52, 64, 70,
    92, 116, 146, 150, 183
Cooley, Harold D., unmailed HST
    letter to, 93–94
Coolidge, Calvin, 61, 149–150
Cooper, John Sherman, 131n16
Cooper, Kent, unmailed HST letter
    to, 11–12
Council of Economic Advisers, 127
Crowley, Leo, 77
Crump, Edward H., 121
Curley, James Michael, 78
Cyrus the Great, of Persia, 138
Czechoslovakia, 33

Daily News. See Chicago *Daily
    News;* Washington *Daily News*
Daily Worker (newspaper), 94
Dallas, C. Donald, 88; unmailed
    HST letter to, 89
Dallas *News,* 10

Dana, Charles Anderson, 168
Daniel, Margaret Truman, 8, 61–
  62, 86, 105, 152; musical career
  of, 3, 173–177, 178
Daniels, Jonathan, unmailed HST
  letter to, 76–77
Darius I, emperor of Persia, 27,
  146
Davies, Joseph, 33
Davis, Bill, 77
Davis, George, unmailed HST
  letter to, 178
Day, J. Edward, unmailed HST
  letter to, 183–184
Dayton, Ohio, 100–101
Death of a President (Manchester),
  168
Democratic Party, HST's views on,
  108–137, 147–149
Dever, Paul A., 124
Dewey, Bradley, 77, unmailed
  HST letter to, 78
Dewey, Thomas E.: 1948 election,
  10, 14, 15, 69, 94, 112, 133;
  1950 election, 117; 1952 election,
  127
Dickens, Charles, 179
Dixiecrats, 62, 102, 105, 112, 120,
  121, 166
Donahue, J. Joseph ("Jiggs"),
  unmailed HST letter to, 129
Dougherty, D. Cardinal, unmailed
  HST letter to, 175
Douglas, William O., unmailed
  HST letter to, 81–82
Drummond, Burt, unmailed HST
  letter to, 20
Duncan, Dick, 62
Durante, Jimmy, 157
Dye, Russell V., 184; unmailed
  HST letter to, 185

Early, Steve, 153
Earnest, Hazel, 53; unmailed HST
  letter to, 52
Earnest, Robert, 51–52
Eastland, James O., 131
Eberhart, Laura (Mrs. W. B.;
  HST's aunt), 141
Economy Act of 1952, 72
Einstein, Albert, 161

Eisenhower, Dwight D., 34, 36, 56,
  105, 132, 139, 167; and
  McCarthyism, 20, 115–116; 1952
  election, 54, 119, 125, 127; 1956
  election, 128–131; unmailed
  HST letter to, 131–132
Eisenhower, John, 131
Ellender, Senator Allen J., 62
Ellis, Hugh C., 149–150; unmailed
  HST letter to, 150
Estonia, 39
Ethiopia, 27
Ethridge, Mark, 39n6
Euphrates Valley, 27
Examiner. See Independence,
  Missouri, *Examiner*

Fair Deal, 94, 96, 97, 102
Fallon, George H., unmailed HST
  letter to, 45
Faneuil Hall (Boston), 78
Federal Aid to Education Bill of
  1949, 98
Federal Deposit Insurance
  Corporation (FDIC), 75
Feis, Herbert, 32; unmailed HST
  letter to, 34
Ferguson, Homer, 74, 80n8
Fillmore, Millard, 131
Fineberg, Abe, unmailed HST
  letter to, 155
Finland, 33
Fitzpatrick, Martin A., unmailed
  HST letter to, 125–126
Fitzpatrick, Paul E., unmailed
  HST letter to, 117–118
Flynn, Ed, 117, 118
Foley, Mrs. Robert T., unmailed
  HST letter to, 159–160
Ford, Henry, 143
Foreign Affairs Quarterly, 60
Formosa, 22, 50
Forrestal, James V., 77
Fortune (magazine), 26
Foy, Eddie, 157
France, 33, 50, 58, 59
Freeman, Douglas, 152

Gallup, George, 90, 91
Gannett newspapers, 9, 113
Garner, John, 113

Gates, John, 94–95; unmailed HST
    letter to, 95–96
Gauss, William P., 129; unmailed
    HST letter to, 130
George, Walter, 74
Germany: Berlin blockade/airlift,
    50, 57, 153; postwar, 33, 37, 40,
    41; in World War II, 36–37
Globe. See Boston Globe
Globe-Democrat. See St. Louis
    Globe-Democrat
Gooch, Congressman Daniel W.,
    152
Grady, Henry F., 45–47; unmailed
    HST letter to, 47–48
Graham, Philip L., 20; unmailed
    HST letters to, 21–22, 56,
    127–128, 177
Graham, Brigadier General
    Wallace H. (White House
    physician), 13
Grande, Richard, unmailed HST
    letter to, 161–162
Grandview, Missouri, 11, 140, 154
Grant, Ulysses S., 135, 148
Greece, 42, 46, 57, 58, 153;
    unmailed HST letter to king and
    queen of, 42
Greeley, Horace, 64, 168
Green, Theodore F., 78; unmailed
    HST letter to, 79
Green, William, 31
Greene, Ward, unmailed HST letter
    to, 25
Gregory, Edmund B., 66, 67
Guam, 59
Guffey, Joe, 78
Gunn, Glenn Dillard, 177
Gustavus, Adolphus, king of
    Sweden, 139

Hadrian, emperor of Rome, 27
Hale, Robert, unmailed HST letter
    to, 51
Hannibal, 138, 139
Harlamert, Irvin H., unmailed
    HST letter to, 44
Harriman, W. Averell, 124, 176
Harriman, W. L., unmailed HST
    letter to, 126
Harrison, Benjamin, 27, 148

Harrison, William Henry, 135
Hassett, Bill, 102
Hearst, William Randolph, 18, 21,
    22, 23, 24, 64, 113, 126, 142,
    168
Hearst newspapers, 9, 10, 16, 19,
    23, 127
Heinrich, Marilyn M., unmailed
    HST letter to, 99
Henry IV, king of France, 145
Herald. See Miami Herald
Hillman, Sidney, 31
Hiroshima, 34–35
Hiss, Alger, 19
Hitler, Adolf, 36, 146
Holding Company Act, 82–83
Holland, Senator Spessard L., 131
Holmes, John J., unmailed HST
    letter to, 25
Holmes, Oliver Wendell, Jr., 157
Hoover, Herbert, 29, 54, 70, 71,
    112, 139, 147
House Agricultural Committee, 93
House Committee on Education
    and Labor, 98
House Committee on Un-American
    Activities, 95
Howard, Roy, 19, 21–22, 56, 120
Hudner, Thomas J., 164
Hughes, Charles E., 68, 69
Hume, Paul, 3, 7n2, 174–175, 177
Humphrey, Hubert, 59
Hungary, 12
Hungry Horse Dam (Montana),
    125
Hunyadi, John, 145

Ickes, Harold, 77
Independence, Missouri, 10, 50,
    83, 140, 154–155, 160, 163,
    171–172, 180–181, 183, 186;
    see also Truman Library
Independence, Missouri,
    Examiner, 17
Independence Hall (Philadelphia),
    78
Indochina, 33, 47, 58–60
Indonesia, 33
Internal Revenue Service, 74–75
International Mark Twain Society,
    29

Interstate Commerce Commission, 73
Iran, 39, 40, 44–47, 153, 176
Irving, Henry, 144
Israel, 43, 47
Italy, 33, 44
Iturbi, Jose, 157–158
Ivan the Terrible, czar of Russia, 50

Jackson, Andrew, 23, 133, 134, 135, 165, 166
Jackson, Robert H., 68
Jackson, Thomas ("Stonewall"), 139
Jackson County, Missouri, 17–18, 85, 86, 87, 137, 142, 183
Japan, 40, 58, 87; atomic bomb and, 4, 32, 34–36
Jeffers, Bill, 78
Jefferson, Thomas, 23
Jeffreys, George, 74n5
Jenner, Senator William E., 126
Johnson, Alvanley, 110
Johnson, Andrew, 152
Johnson, Louis, 49
Johnson, Lyndon B., 59, 168, 169
Jones, Jesse, 22
Jones, Merle S., 163; unmailed HST letter to, 164
Judd, Walter, 22

Kansas City, Missouri, 10, 86, 100, 101, 110–112, 140–144, 154, 177–179
Kansas City Club, 177–178
Kansas City *Star,* 18, 22, 64, 112, 137, 140, 150–151
Kansas-Nebraska Bill, 135
Kefauver, Estes: 1952 election, 119, 121, 124; 1956 election, 128–129
Kemper, Rufus Crosby, 136; unmailed HST letter to, 137
Kemper, William, 143
Kennedy, Jacqueline, 169
Kennedy, John F., 58, 98–99, 108, 136, 181; death of, 4, 168–169; 1960 election, 132–133, 134, 166
Kennedy, Joseph, 134

Kennedy or Nixon . . . (Schlesinger), 166, 167
Kent, Frank, 112, 114; unmailed HST letters to, 24, 113–114
Key West, Florida, 28–29, 111, 171, 173
Kiel Canal, 27, 40
Kimbrell, Raymond B., 63; unmailed HST letter to, 64
Kintner, Robert, 165
Klemm, Karl, 143
Knight, Jack, 19, 21
Knowland, William F., 22, 120, 122
Know Nothing Party, 131
Kohlberg, Alfred, 83
Korea, 40, 47; *see also* Korean war
Korean war, 23, 49–57, 59, 93, 102, 144–145, 153
Krock, Arthur, 26; unmailed HST letters to, 27–28, 57–58
Kupcinet, Irv, unmailed HST letter to, 35–36

Latvia, 33, 39
Lawrence, David, 122
Leahy, William, 13, 33, 172
Lee, Robert E., 139, 147, 152
Lenin, Nikolai, 50
Lesinski, John, unmailed HST letter to, 98
Lewis, Fulton, Jr., 25, 64
Lewis, John L., 31, 32, 110
Lhevinne, Josef, 144
Lieberson, Goddard, unmailed HST letter to, 146–147
Life (magazine), 23, 64, 162, 173
Lincoln, Abraham, 23, 133
Lithuania, 33, 39
Littell, Norman, unmailed HST letter to, 145–146
Long, Edward V., 182
Look (magazine), 130, 161, 162
Los Angeles *News,* 174
Los Angeles *Times,* 10
Louis, Joe, 78
Lovett, Robert A., 47, 72
Lowenthal, Max, 82–83
Luce, Henry, 23

MacArthur, Douglas, 49, 52–53,
56, 59, 60; HST fires, 4, 53–56
McCarran, Pat, 74
McCarthy, Joseph R., 19–20, 114–
116, 125, 126; unmailed HST
letter to, 114–115
McCarthyism/McCarthyites,
19–20, 23, 58, 114–116
McClellan, John L., 62, 70, 131;
unmailed HST letter to, 70–71
McCormick, Medill, 64
McCormick, Robert R. ("Bertie"),
14, 18, 21, 22, 23, 113, 120,
125, 142
McCormick newspapers, 9, 10, 16,
23
McKellar, Kenneth, unmailed HST
letter to, 90–91
McKim, Charles F., 61
McKim, Mead and White
(architectural firm), 61
McKinley, William, 27, 148
McKinney, Frank, 123–124
Madison, James, 134
Manchester, William, 168;
unmailed HST letter to,
168–169
Mansfield, Richard, 144
Mantell, Robert Bruce, 144
Mao Tse-tung, 49, 50
Marlowe, Julia, 144
Marshall, George C., 42, 44, 55,
125, 126
Marshall Plan, 42, 58, 153
Martel, Charles, 145
Martin, Joseph, 53, 55
Mead, James M., 66; unmailed
HST letter to, 67
Meade, George, 152
Metropolitan Opera, 143
Meyer, Eugene, 21, 56
Miami *Herald*, 18–19, 21, 120
Middle East, 42–48, 62, 176; *see
also individual countries*
Marcus, Stanley, unmailed HST
letter to, 92–93
Miller, Merle, 164; unmailed HST
letter to, 165
Millikin, Eugene, 74
Missouri Valley Authority, 99–102

Morganthau, Henry J., Jr., 37,
76–77
Morton, Thruston B., 131n16
Mueller, Erwin J., 5–6
Murphy, Charles, 59, 132, 155
Murray, Philip, 31, 110

National Association of Manu-
facturers, 127
National Chamber of Commerce,
127
national health-insurance plan, 5,
88, 96–97
NBC television network, 165
Neiman-Marcus (Dallas), 92
Nelson, James, 165; unmailed HST
letter to, 166
Nelson, William Rockwell, 4, 142,
143
New Deal, 87–88, 94, 99
New Orleans *Times Picayune,* 10
News. See Dallas *News*
News-Press (Kansas City weekly),
18
Newsweek (magazine), 103
New York *Times,* 10, 13–14, 26
New York *World-Telegram,* 19n5
New Yorker, The (magazine),
unmailed HST letter to, 29–30
Nichols, William I., 162; unmailed
HST letter to, 163
Niles, Ray, 178
Nixon, Richard M., 4, 59–60, 131,
134, 166; 1952 election, 120,
125, 126
Nobel, Alfred, 142
Noland, Ethel, 171
North Atlantic Treaty Organization
(NATO), 42, 47, 58
North Korea. *See* Korea; Korean
war
North Vietnam. *See* Vietnam
Noyes, David, 165

Oakes, Grant W., unmailed HST
letter to, 41
O'Connor, Basil, 86
Office of Price Administration
(OPA), 88, 90, 91, 93
Olcott, Chauncey, 143

O'Rourke, John T., 54; unmailed
HST letter to, 55–56
Overton, John H., 62

Pace, Frank, 49
Pachmann, Vladimir de, 144
Pacific Agreement, 58
Paderewski, Ignace Jan, 144
Palestine, 43, 47
Pallette, Mel, 17
Parrish, Wayne W., unmailed
HST letter to, 26
Patterson, Robert P., 34, 125
Patton, James G., unmailed HST
letter to, 91–92
Pauley, Edwin W., 33, 79, 134
Peacock, J. Neely, unmailed HST
letter to, 136
Pearl Harbor, 35–36
Pearson, Drew, 25, 64
Pegler, Westbrook, 25, 83, 161
Pendergast, James, 85n1, 110;
unmailed HST letters to,
110–112
Pendergast, Mike, 85, 86n3
Pendergast, Thomas J. ("Boss"),
86n3, 109, 142, 159
Perkins, Frances, 77
Perlman, Philip B., 80
Perry, Milton, 158, 162
Petrillo, James, 31
Philippines, 33, 58
Pick, Lewis A., 99–100
Pickwick Hotel (Kansas City),
unmailed HST letter to, 179–180
Pierce, Franklin, 135
Pius XII, Pope, 175
Plain Dealer. See Cleveland
Plain Dealer
Plain Speaking (Miller), 164
Poland, 33, 39, 40
Polk, James K., 135
Ponce de Leon, Juan, 114
Ponsi, Charles, 78
Porperi, Guston L., 62
Post. See Washington *Post*
Post-Dispatch. See St. Louis
Post-Dispatch
Potsdam Agreement, 32–33, 36, 37,
40

Primrose and Dockstader
(vaudeville team), 143
Pulitzer, Joseph, 11, 16, 18, 22
Pulitzer newspapers, 9, 10
Pusey, Merlo, unmailed HST
letter to, 68–69

Randall, William, 181; unmailed
HST letter to, 182
Rankin, John, unmailed HST
letter to, 102
Rayburn, Sam, 110, 153, 156;
unmailed HST letter to, 132
Reconstruction Finance
Corporation, 103, 104, 118
Reporter, The (magazine), 23, 24
Republican Party, 10–11, 62–63,
110, 113–114, 125, 148–149
Revercomb, Chapman, 131
Rhine-Danube waterway, 27, 33, 40
Richmond, Virginia, *Times-
Dispatch,* unmailed HST letter
to, 12–13
Ridgway, Matthew B., 52
Roberts, Owen J., 66, 68–69
Roberts, Roy, 22, 119; unmailed
HST letters to, 140–144, 151
Robinson, Jackie, 161
Rockefeller, John D., 142
Ronald, M. B., unmailed HST
letter to, 100–101
Roosevelt, Eleanor, 153; unmailed
HST letter to, 65–66
Roosevelt, Franklin Delano, 16,
22n7, 31, 38, 63, 87, 94, 107,
133, 139, 150, 166–167; last
days of, 153, 171–172; HST's
assessment of cabinet of, 76–77;
1944 election, 151–153
Roosevelt, Franklin D., Jr.,
unmailed HST letter to, 72–73
Roosevelt, Theodore, 27, 61, 133,
148
Roosevelt College (Chicago), 128
Roper, Elmo, 14; unmailed HST
letter to, 15–16
Rosenman, Sam, 150
Rosenthal, Moriz, 144
Ross, Charles, 28, 29, 68, 174
Rumania, 33, 39, 40

Ruml, Beardsley, 124
Russell, Lillian, 143

Sabath, Adolph, unmailed HST
    letter to, 81
Safly, Elizabeth, 7
St. Louis *Globe-Democrat*, 107
St. Louis *Post-Dispatch*, 22
Sale, Chic, 143
Sanford, Seward F., 147; unmailed
    HST letter to, 148-149
San Francisco *Call-Bulletin*, 22
Sarnoff, David, 165
Saturday Evening Post (magazine),
    46, 165
Sawyer, Charles, 47
Schlesinger, Arthur, Jr., 166;
    unmailed HST letter to, 167-168
Schott, Webster, 150-151
Schricker, Henry F., 124n13
Scott, Winfield, 135
Screen Gems, 165, 166
Scripps-Howard newspapers, 9, 19,
    22, 127
Shipley, Ruth B., unmailed HST
    letter to, 82-83
Slaughter, Roger C., 110-111
Sloan, W. G., 99-100
Smalley, Garrett, 18; unmailed
    HST letter to, 19
Smith, Harold, 77
Smith, Willis, 74
Snyder, John, 13, 73, 78
Sokolsky, George, 161
"Solomon Wise" (newspaper
    column), 17
Sothern, Edward, 144
South Africa, 47
South America, 27
Southern, William M., Jr., 16-17;
    unmailed HST letter to, 17-18
South Korea. *See* Korea; Korean
    war
South Vietnam. *See* Vietnam
space race. *See* Sputnik
Sparkman, John, 108, 121;
    unmailed HST letter to, 122-123
Spottswood, John, 173-174
Sputnik/space race, 98
Squire, Jack, unmailed HST letter
    to, 130

Stalin, Joseph, 10, 32, 33, 36, 50,
    114
Star. See Kansas City *Star;*
    Washington *Star*
Stark, Lloyd, 107
Stassen, Harold E., unmailed HST
    letter to, 54
Stettinius, Edward Reilley, 76
Stevenson, Adlai E., 106, 107-108;
    1952 election, 119-125, 127;
    1956 election, 128-129; unmailed
    HST letters to, 120-121, 123-125
Stimson, Henry L., 34, 77
Stone, Harlan F., 68
Story, Bill, 185
Stover, Mrs. Russell, unmailed
    HST letter to, 178-179
Stuart, J. E. B., 139
Sudan, 47
Suez Canal, 33
Sullivan, Mark, 113, 114
Sulzberger, Arthur, unmailed HST
    letter to, 13-14
Sun Times. See Chicago *Sun Times*
Surplus Property Program/Act,
    66-67
Susskind, David, 164, 165
Sweden, 145-146
Swoyer, Martha Ann, 140n1, 186
Sylva, Marguerita, 143
Symington, Stuart, 133; unmailed
    HST letters to, 118-119, 181-182

Taft, Robert A., unmailed HST
    letter to, 119-120
"Talk of the Town" (*New Yorker*
    column), 29
Talmadge, Herman, 131
Taylor, J. E. ("Buck"), 118
Taylor, Zachary, 131, 135
television, HST and, 163-166
Tennessee Valley Authority
    (TVA), 99, 131
Terry, Ellen, 144
This Week (magazine), 162, 163
Thomas, Lowell, unmailed HST
    letter to, 176
Thomas, R. J., 31
Thurmond, Strom, 112, 131
Time (magazine), 23, 64, 68, 102,
    162, 163, 173

Times. See Los Angeles *Times;*
New York *Times*
Times-Dispatch. See Richmond,
Virginia, *Times-Dispatch*
Times-Herald. See Washington
Times-Herald.
Times Picayune. See New Orleans
Times Picayune
Tobey, Charles W., unmailed HST
letter to, 103–104
Tobin, Dan, 31
Townsend, Francis E., 78
Transportation Act of 1940, 83
Tribune. See Chicago *Tribune*
Truman, Bess, 152, 171, 177–179;
unmailed HST letters to, 172–
173, 186
Truman, Harry S.: and atomic
bomb, 4, 26, 32, 34–36;
communism, 11–12, 19–20, 26–
27, 114–115, 144–145; early
years, 10–11, 112, 138–144, 162,
170–171; economic policies of,
87–94; and foreign affairs, 11,
19, 38–48, 53, 57–60 (*see also*
Korean war, *below*); and
national health-insurance plan,
5, 88, 96–97; and history, 145–
149, 152, 162, 165–168 (*see also*
views of presidency and past
presidents, *below*); interior
programs of, 99–102, 104–106;
and Jackson County, Missouri,
politics, 17–18, 85–86, 97, 112,
137, 142; and Korean war, 23,
49–57, 59, 93, 102, 144–145,
153; and labor unions, 31–32,
81, 87, 110, 121; and Mac-
Arthur firing, 4, 53–56; and
music career of Margaret
Truman, 4, 173–178; and 1948
election, 10, 14, 16, 19, 64, 69,
112, 133; and the press, 3–4,
9–30, 113 (*see also specific
publications and newsmen*);
relations with Congress, 51,
62–67, 69–83, 90–94, 97–98;
retirement of, 30, 56, 83, 119,
150, 178–186; role in 1952 and
1956 elections, 54, 106–108,
119–129; and television, 163–

166; temper of, 3–4, 7, 25, 56,
82, 120–121, 184 (and *passim*);
and Truman Library, 4–5, 6, 7,
114, 137, 154–163, 180–181,
185–186; and U.S. Supreme
Court, 4, 68–69, 81–82, 104–106;
as Vice-President and first days
of presidency, 18, 38, 107, 109,
151–153, 171–173; view of
presidency and past presidents,
8, 23, 61, 76–77, 131, 133–137,
139, 148–150, 168–169; and
World War II and settlement,
32–37, 40, 50, 65
Truman, John (HST's uncle), 141
Truman, Margaret. *See* Daniel,
Margaret Truman
Truman, Martha (HST's mother),
11, 138, 139
Truman, Mary Jane (HST's
sister), 154, 172, 174
Truman, Ralph (HST's cousin),
114
Truman, Vivian (HST's brother),
154
Truman Doctrine, 42, 46
Truman Library, 4–5, 6, 7, 114,
137, 154–159, 160–163, 180–
181, 185–186
Tugwell, Rexford Guy, 167;
unmailed HST letter to, 115
Tunisia, 47
Turkey, 40–42, 57, 58, 153
Turoff, Ben, unmailed HST letter
to, 96–97
Twain, Mark, 29–30
Tydings, Millard, unmailed HST
letter to, 80
Tyler, John, 135

United Farm Equipment and
Metal Workers Union, 41
United Kingdom, 42, 50, 59; and
Middle East, 45–47
United Nations, 43, 45, 153; and
Korean war, 49, 50, 51, 53
United Press, 22
U.S.S.R.: and propaganda, 11–12;
and atomic bomb, 26; U.S.
relations with, 32–33, 36–37,
40–42; foreign ministers

U.S.S.R. (Cont.)
conference (1945), 38–41; and
Korean war, 50, 53, 56, 144–
146; and Middle East, 44–45;
space program, 98; World War
II settlement, 32–33, 36, 37, 40
U.S. Supreme Court, 4, 68–69,
74n6, 81–82, 104, 105, 106
U.S.S. *Williamsburg* (presidential
yacht), 39

Vaccaro, Tony, unmailed HST
letter to, 28–29
Van Buren, Martin, 134–135
Vandenberg, Arthur H., 172
Vardaman, James K., Jr., 79
Vatican City, 44
Victoria, queen of England, 27
Vietnam, 58–60
Vinson, Fred M., 68, 77
Voice of America, 11
Vrooman, Howard J., 85

Wade, Ben, 152
Wake Island, 53, 59
Walker, Frank, 77
Wallace, Henry, 77, 172
Wallgren, Mon, 79–80, 81, 185
Walling, L. Metcalfe, 79
Washington, George, 23, 149
Washington *Daily News*, 54
Washington *Post*, 3, 20, 21, 56,
68, 174–177
Washington *Star*, 24, 113
Washington *Times-Herald*, 177

Weatherford, Bob, 50, 146, 154
Weber and Fields (vaudeville
team), 143
Webster Quimmly Society, unsent
HST telegram to, 116
Westwood, Mike, 5n1
Wheeler, Burton K., 72, 82;
unmailed HST letter to, 73–74
Wherry, Kenneth S., 67, 114n8
White, Mrs. E. C., 141
White House, 61, 78, 79, 158–159,
172
Whiteway, Stanley E., 155;
unmailed HST letter to, 156–157
Whitney, Alexander F., 110
Wickard, Claude R., 77
Williams, John J., 122
Williams and Walker (vaudeville
team), 143
Wills, Nat, 143
Wilson, Woodrow, 23, 133, 148
Winchell, Walter, 25, 64
Woodward, Stanley, 13
World-Telegram. See New York
World-Telegram
World War II, 36–37, 65; and
atomic bomb, 4, 32, 34–36;
Potsdam Agreement, 32–33, 36,
37, 40
Wornall, John, 141
Wyatt, Wilson, 124, 125

Xerxes, 146

Yalu River, 53

DATE DUE

The Library Store   #47-0106

Strictly personal & confidential
HST.